# Iron Roads to the Far North & Kyle

A travellers and tourists guide to the Inverness to Wick & Thurso and Kyle of Lochalsh lines

## Michael Pearson

www.wayzgoose.org.uk
Tel: 01283 713674 / 821472
Copyright: Michael Pearson
All Rights Reserved.
First Edition 2003  ISBN 0 907864 98 8
Printed in Italy by STIGE Via Pescarito
110 10099 San Mauro Torino

**WAYZGOOSE**

**Tomich** - 'Safeway Flyer'.

# NORTH & WEST OF INVERNESS

Ben Griam Mor

Attadale

'SORRY to wake you. Yes, I know it's only four, but I thought you'd like to see the timber train.'

Rogart's coming to with a refreshing shower; the gentle drizzle which wakes up the majority of its summer mornings.

'Here, I'll carry the teas on to the platform.'

There's a thrush singing on the lamp-post. In the field beside the river the cattle are shaking their dewy flanks. The vanillary smell of broom anticipates the croissants to come. Two buzzards are wheeling over the conifer plantation, and an oystercatcher is piping its way along the Fleet.

'The seats are too damp to sit on. We'll walk up to the end of the platform. The train won't be long.'

You try to extract the sound of it, coming up the valley, from all the other sounds that the world generates naturally before man noisily makes his entrance. The strath plays tricks with you, magnifying some sounds, dampening others; water amplifies, wood muffles. The Fleet, rushing over its rocky bed, is teasingly going through its routine of goods train imitations.

'There it is. Listen!'

And yes, that is a new noise, a common time rhythm of four-wheeled wagons hitting rail joints. Thump, thump, thump, thump - thump, thump, thump, thump. But then it goes again, as softly as it came, and that thrush still sings its merry harmony, and you glance at your watch and it reads four-thirty, and you wonder if there's been a glitch, but you know they can't afford to have one, because the timber train has got to be clear of the line for the first passenger trains of the day.

But then you hear it again, and this time you're sure, as proof comes positive with a plaintive blast on the locomotive's horn which echoes back and forth across the strath, oscillating off the ridges like a piper's lament. And the train bends into view, its headlight gilding the damp sleepers and the wet rails, a mechanical giant with this Cyclopean eye, hypnotising you with its intensity.

The train enters the loop and slows for the unguarded crossing. You can make out the driver now, behind the raindrops on his windscreen, quietly confident at his controls in charge of twenty lorries worth of freshly cut timber giving off an aromatic resinous odour which could be bottled and sold as shower gel.

'This is what I wanted you to see. How four hundred tons of freight can be moved in a manner at harmony with the environment. Not only are twenty lorries being kept off the narrow Highland roads, each time the timber train runs, its journey generates an aura all its own. For line-side dwellers it book-ends the day: telling them its time for bed as it runs up Strath Ullie of an evening; waking them up on the shores of Cromarty Firth on its loaded return. Similarly, the 'Safeway Flyer', the overnight express which brings supermarket goods up from the outskirts of Glasgow at speeds a lorry couldn't legally match, saves its own coterie from the rigidity of Greenwich Mean Time.'

'You see what I mean? Good. We can go back to bed now!'

Go back to bed and think about the Far North Line, and its off-shoot to Kyle. How would the Highlands be without them? How would remote

Helmsdale

communities like Rogart be without a railway on their doorstep? As far back as the 1930s the London Midland & Scottish Railway compiled reports to see if money might be saved by abandoning all their routes north of Perth. Thirty years later - and despite the fact that the Second World War might have been considerably harder to win without the transportation input of the Far North and Kyle lines - Doctor Beeching was recommending their closure. Both routes survived by the skin of their teeth, but in 1971 the Government consented to British Railways proposal that the Dingwall to Kyle of Lochalsh line should close, a closure largely instigated by the fact that the Government had previously announced that no further grants towards the cost of retaining the Kyle line would be made.

This tends to be our way with railways in Britain. Myopically, we see them as issues pertaining to profit and loss, and not as strategic lines of communication. Because they were built with investment capital we define them as going concerns, businesses which must at best return a healthy profit, or at worst break even. Do roads and hospitals and opera-houses make a profit? It's from a misplaced perception that railways suffer by comparison. How did the Department of Transport spend taxpayer's money? They subsidised railways and invested in roads. The semantic variance in definition emphasises the dichotomy that lies at the misaligned centre of our inability to promote and maintain a truly integrated transport system.

Inadvertently, the Energy Crisis of 1973 saved the Kyle line from a second real threat of closure. Lord Carrington's proposal that an oil rig construction yard at Drumbie be taken into public ownership, and the need to transport heavy materials unsuitable for consignment by road, saw the line being retained into a more sanguine era where a broader consensus viewed railways in a wider context, valuing them for their environmentally cohesive contribution to the economy as a whole.

Such revisionism wasn't brought about organically. It needed championing. For every Roundhead there had to be a Cavalier, for every Richard Beeching there had to be a Frank Spaven. When Frank Spaven died at the age of 85 in January 2003, his obituary in 'The Herald' speculated that this first head of planning at the Highlands and Islands Development Board, kirk elder and inveterate walker, had been instrumental in saving the bulk of the Highland rail network from closure. It noted the unsentimental and fluid style in which he presented cogent arguments for retention of the Highland rail system. 'Spaven dismissed sentiment, rather highlighting the key role of railways as a green and civilised form of transport', 'The Herald' concluded.

That Spaven loved railways for their own sake is widely known - 'as a boy he watched trains from a signal box in East Lothian', 'The Herald' informed - but he had the sense to cloak his affection from the Philistines who would ridicule such a boyish outlook. Fellow travellers - in more ways than one - we who would support the long-term retention and development of a Highland railway network can only salute Frank Spaven's contribution, and to his memory this volume is humbly dedicated.

MICHAEL PEARSON

Highland Rail Partnership and Wayzgoose gratefully acknowledge the financial support of these companies, organisations and individuals in the production of this guide book.

EWS is Britain's leading rail freight operator. Trains serve almost every part of the rail network in Britain and provide continental and international links through ports and the Channel Tunnel. EWS moves over 100 million tonnes of freight every year and operates over 1,500 trains every weekday. EWS has invested over £750 million in rail freight facilities, including developing the Class 66 locomotive which has become the form for freight traction across Europe and ordering over 3,000 new wagons.

EWS operates daily services to and from the Highlands. EWS is unique in its ability to offer customers integrated trains, allowing them to have their goods arrive at a predetermined time without having to book a complete train. Rail freight is growing quickly in the Highlands and companies are using the rail network where it is sensible to do so to provide reliability and improvements in speed. Most high street chains are now using EWS rail freight services at some point on journeys for their distribution requirements.

The Council's Planning & Development Service provides direct advice & financial help to businesses, supports community-led projects and participates in multi-partnership initiatives as part of an integrated approach to economic development within the Highlands.

The Friends of the Far North Line is the campaign group for rail north of Inverness, lobbying for improved services for local users, tourists and freight. Its 1995 Conference for rail interests was the precursor of the Highland Rail Partnership. Achievements include the Easter Ross commuter services, Beauly station, all-line winter Sunday trains, and initiating the re-introduction of significant freight. It aims to work in partnerships, publishes a thrice-yearly newsletter, and is democratically governed through its AGM and geographically representative committee. It offers membership at £7 - Tel: 01334 475311.

## FRIENDS OF THE KYLE LINE

The Friends of the Kyle Line were formed in 1995 after doubts were once again raised about the future of the rail service on the Kyle Line. They currently have a gift shop, museum, and informal information service at Kyle station which is open daily from 11.20 to 17.15, Sundays excepted. The Friends have promoted steam specials to Kyle and would hope to make steam a regular feature on the line. They are currently working with ScotRail to promote the existing Kyle Line services to visitors in the area. Telephone 01599 534824 for membership or other information.

## SMALL STATIONS SOCIETY

The Small Stations Society exists to support Britain's smallest railway stations, to encourage their maintenance, and present them in the best possible way to the travelling public.

The aim of Caithness and Sutherland Enterprise (CASE), which covers the largest of the ten local enterprise company areas in the Highlands and Islands Enterprise network is to realise the full potential of the people in Caithness and Sutherland.

All efforts towards achieving this aim are focussed upon three objectives - strengthening communities, developing skills, growing businesses and global connections. These objectives are interlinked and we strive to ensure that the projects we are involved in are economically, socially and environmentally sustainable. While we have a remit to promote prosperity today, we also have an obligation to protect our unique environmental and cultural legacy for future generations.

Ross and Cromarty Enterprise (RACE) is one of ten Local Enterprise Companies in the Highlands and Islands Enterprise (HIE) network. We are the principal development agency in the area which covers almost half a million hectares, from east coast to west coast, and has a population of over 50,000.

At RACE we provide a wide range of services designed to help people improve the quality of life in Ross and Cromarty. These services - which range from confidential advice to financial support - are intended to help individuals, business and communities to realise their full potential.

Our vision is to help make Ross and Cromarty the best place to live and work in the Highlands of Scotland. Our services are aligned under three strategic objectives: strengthening communities, developing skills and growing businesses. In pursuing these objectives, we take account of a number of important issues including the need to prioritise how we use limited resources. Our company ethos also embraces various values such as sustainability, partnership, inclusion, risk-taking and innovation. Our priority areas for development in Ross and Cromarty include South West Ross, the Seaboard areas of East Ross including Cromarty, and areas of relatively high unemployment such as Alness, Invergordon and Milton. Key sectors for targeting economic development opportunities include knowledge and information technology, manufacturing, food and drink, sustainable technology and tourism.

The Highland Rail Partnership is an association of Highland Council, Perth & Kinross Council, Argyll & Bute Council, ScotRail, Network Rail, EWS, Freightliner, West Coast Railway Company, Argyll and the Isles Enterprise, Ross & Cromarty Enterprise, Caithness & Sutherland Enterprise, Moray Badenoch & Strathspey Enterprise and the Friends of the Kyle, Far North and West Highland lines. The Partnership aims to assist the development of passenger, freight and heritage rail business across the Highland area.

The Station Tearoom & Craft Shop was established in 1992 in the old waiting rooms of Dingwall Station. We serve quality home baking, speciality soups and light lunches all day. The Craft Shop has locally made products, paintings by local artists, childrens toys and books.

With 114 stores, Safeway is the market leader in Scotland and the fourth largest retailer in the UK. Environmental issues are very important at Safeway. As part of its drive to cut air and noise pollution, Safeway has turned to the railway to help it transport its daily deliveries of fresh foods to its Scottish stores at Inverness, Elgin, Thurso, Wick, Nairn, Buckie and Kirkwall. Transporting some 10 tonnes per day. Safeway is the only retailer in Scotland to carry goods by rail. This pioneering service has been awarded the "Queen's Award for Enterprise".

**sleeperzzz.com**

Recreating the camping coach tradition, owner Kate Roach welcomes travellers from all over the world to the two Mark 2 First Class coaches and 127 DMU which are stabled in the sidings at Rogart Station, halfway between Inverness and Wick. Each carriage sleeps 8 with two beds per compartment, plus kitchen, sitting room, dining room and toilets/showers.

Rogart is a tranquil crofting village 4 miles from the coast and has a shop and pub/restaurant. Sample whisky, visit Dunrobin Castle, see the salmon leap or walk across the hills. Come and unwind for a night or a week - call 01408 641343.

Network Rail is an engineering company committed to revitalising Britain's railways. We maintain, improve and upgrade every aspect of the railway infrastructure. We are clearly focussed on the operation, maintenance and renewal of the railway and intend to apply engineering excellence to make the railway fit for the long-term.

Network Rail will invest £300 million in Scotland this year and by improving the infrastructure of the railway we will create a safe and efficient rail industry that the public can depend on.

In addition, there are wider benefits to society and the environment to be gained by delivering an effective national rail network, which supports the delivery of an integrated and socially inclusive transport system.

Dunrobin Castle, home of the Clan Sutherland, dates from the early 14th Century. The castle contains an outstanding collection of paintings, furniture, tapestries and silver. There are also magnificent formal gardens and informative falconry displays. The Museum contains Pictish stone and big game trophies. Gift shop and tea-room. Open 1st April - 15th October. Tel: 01408 633177. Fax 01408 634081. email info@dunrobincastle.net

The Highland Council is one of 32 unitary councils in Scotland, providing a wide range of essential services to a population of 210,000 people. The area covered by the council is 10,000 square miles - one third of the area of mainland Scotland.. The council has the largest area of any council in Scotland and is one of the largest in Europe. This large area gives the council major responsibilities for land, air and sea transport. The Highland railways make an important contribution to the integrated transport network of sparsely populated rural communities and also provide important links to the remainder of Scotland and the UK.

ScotRail is Scotland's national passenger train operator, providing over 95% of services north of the border. We run four types of service - urban commuter services around Glasgow and Edinburgh; interurban express services linking Scotland's six cities (Glasgow, Edinburgh, Dundee, Aberdeen, Inverness and Stirling); rural routes in Dumfries and Galloway, the West Highlands and the lines described in this book; and the Caledonian Sleepers which link Inverness, Aberdeen, Fort William, Glasgow and Edinburgh direct with London. The Glasgow suburban network supported by Strathclyde Passenger Transport is the largest in Britain outside London. In April 1997 the National Express Group commenced a seven-year franchise for ScotRail during which it has invested over £200M in new and refurbished trains. In May 2000 we transferred to the Kyle and Far North Lines our 90 mph Class 158 trains which have several advantages for passenger comfort including two toilets and air-conditioning and have recently received investment supported by the Strategic Rail Authority to improve their performance. We also introduced without external support a commuter service in March 1998 from Dingwall which was extended in September 2000 to Tain, some through running between these lines and the Central Belt or Aberdeen, and with the support of the Highland Rail Partnership a first-ever all-year Sunday service to/from Kyle and from/to the Far North. We have introduced flexipass fares for commuting into Inverness and Apex fares bookable up to two days in advance for travel between Wick, Thurso, Kyle of Lochalsh or Dingwall and Aberdeen, Glasgow or Edinburgh, and have raised the discount for ticket purchases with the Highland Railcard from 33 to 50%. Cycles now go free on ScotRail subject to advance reservation on these routes. Our ScotRail Shortbreak holidays include hotels in Inverness, Kyle of Lochalsh, Dornoch, Ullapool, Thurso and Wick, and both the Freedom of Scotland Travelpass and the Highland Rover tickets now give a 30% discount on Northlink Ferries between Scrabster and Stromness as well as inclusive bus travel Thurso-Scrabster (the Travelpass also offers free bus travel Wick/Thurso-John o'Groats, Inverness-Ullapool and Kyle-Uig). In April 2002 we experimentally opened the new station at Beauly - we are also the operator of all the other stations on both routes, and are working to improve them in conjunction with the Highland Rail Partnership and other stakeholders.

HRP and Wayzgoose also gratefully recognise the financial support for this project of two private individuals: Geoffrey Evison and John Yellowlees.

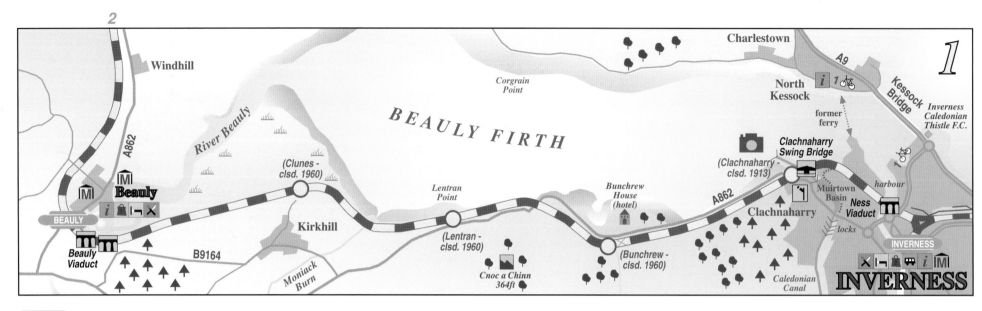

Windhill

*River Beauly*

**Beauly**

BEAULY

Beauly
Viaduct

A862

B9164

Kirkhill

*Moniack
Burn*

*(Clunes -
clsd. 1960)*

*Lentran
Point*

*(Lentran -
clsd. 1960)*

Cnoc a Chinn
364ft

*Corgrain
Point*

B E A U L Y   F I R T H

*Bunchrew
House
(hotel)*

*(Bunchrew -
clsd. 1960)*

Charlestown

A9

North
Kessock

*former
ferry*

*Kessock
Bridge*

*Inverness
Caledonian
Thistle F.C.*

**Clachnaharry
Swing Bridge**

*(Clachnaharry -
clsd. 1913)*

A862

**Clachnaharry**

Muirtown
Basin

*Ness
Viaduct*

*harbour*

*locks*

*Caledonian
Canal*

INVERNESS

**INVERNESS**

**M** ORE like a theatre foyer than a station concourse, the circulating area beyond the buffer stops at INVERNESS station bristles with anticipation. Surely no other railway station in the United Kingdom can offer such a multiplicity of scenic routes to explore. No wonder intending passengers bear the demeanour of theatre-goers anticipating the curtain about to rise on an entertaining adventure.

Aficionados of the Far North and Kyle lines ensconce themselves, if at all feasible, on the right hand side of the train. They know where the best views lie! Despite its recently found city status, Inverness is soon left astern. But first look out for the sidings where the Safeway container train is unloaded early each morning, a modern success story for EWS specifically and rail freight in general. These truncated spurs are all that remain of the Harbour Branch which once extended to the riverbank itself, to facilitate transhipment of goods between rail and sea.

The original masonry Ness Viaduct of 1862 came to sudden grief in February 1989 when it was swept away by floods. For over a year the Far North and Kyle routes were separated from the rest of the railway network, but British Rail determinedly operated their services in isolation. When the new bridge was opened by Malcolm Rifkind in May 1990 the management demanded to know of its driver why his train was fifteen months late. As you cross its modern replacement, watch out for any coastal vessels unloading in the harbour precincts. Like the Safeway train, it's good to see modes other than road being used to carry freight. But in the background the Kessock Bridge of 1982 reminds us that road now holds most of the aces where transport in Britain is concerned! Authorisation for a branch to the Caledonian Canal's Muirtown Basin was authorised in 1890. The trouble was the line had been laid thirteen years previously and the Highland Railway had inadvertently omitted to obtain official sanction for the line!

No sooner has your train apparently got into its stride, than it slows to a walking pace to cross the Caledonian Canal. There aren't many regularly operated railway swing-bridges in Britain, but two of them span either end of Telford's famous canal: one on the west coast at Banavie on the West Highland line: the other here, at CLACHNAHARRY, where the canal joins the Beauly Firth. This Clachnaharry swing-bridge is a wonderful contraption, very much in the British tradition of engineering genius seasoned with eccentricity. It spans the canal between its entrance lock and a second lock which lifts the level of the water up into Muirtown's broad basin, filled largely with pleasure craft these days, though fishing vessels do still use the canal. The swing-bridge is 126 feet long and pivots from the southern bank. A bridge-keeper cum signalman occupies the tiny Highland Railway signal cabin overlooking it, the sole remaining operational mechanical box in the radio-controlled zone north of Inverness. It's a great pity that Clachnaharry station closed before the Great War, for passengers of a mechanical bent would doubtless welcome the opportunity to alight here and inspect the swing-bridge and hopefully witness its operational procedure. Ascertaining from radio headquarters at Inverness that no trains are due, the keeper manually unlocks the bridge and releases a positioning bar before proceeding to a control panel located on the seaward girder of the bridge. In order to swing the structure, the decking is first hydraulically lifted to clear the approach rails, before lowering to be swung. The whole process takes around four minutes to complete and draws intense interest from spectators, notably the crews of vessels making a passage along the canal. British Waterways have made a killing on visitors to the Falkirk Wheel. Clachnaharry Swing-bridge is a gentle reminder that small can also be beautiful, and that popularity is vulgar.

The Inverness & Ross-shire Railway's were not the first rails to be laid at Clachnaharry. In 1804 an iron railway of indeterminate gauge was built to facilitate construction of the Caledonian Canal between the sea lock and Muirtown Basin. Making the sea lock itself was no easy project. Beauly Firth's shoreline slopes gradually, and the entrance lock had to be at least four hundred yards from the land to ensure a sufficient depth of water existed to enable shipping to enter or leave at any state of the tide. Telford's men hammered an iron bar into the mud and it sank fifty-five feet before encountering the sea bed. A massive clay embankment was driven out into the firth to provide a solid foundation for the canal. Take stock while you can. We are surrounded by achievement and beauty, but the majority of folk on the train will be listening to piffle on their personal stereos or have their head down in pulp fiction.

Between Clachnaharry and Clunes the track was double from 1914 until 1966. For a time there was an unusual section of gauntleted track beyond the north end of the platform at Clachnaharry. There were stations at Bunchrew, Lentran and Clunes, all closing to passenger traffic on 13th June, 1960 and goods four years later. By then buses could take the locals into Inverness more expeditiously. Now, as queues build up at the bottleneck overbridge at Clachnaharry, transport planners have cause to regret such closures.

Beauly Firth is as beautiful as its name suggests. The railway hugs the shore. Herons on the look out for their fish supper pay no heed to passing trains. On the far bank lies the Black Isle, neither black nor an island, but rather an intensively farmed peninsular. At Bunchrew the little pink station building remains intact, domestically used now, as is a neighbouring chapel executed in the same stone. Bunchrew's level crossing was the very first un-gated, un-barriered crossing to be opened on the British Rail network. Beyond the site of Clunes station, which served the village of Kirkhill, the railway veers inland, growing more pastoral in nature, with butterbur and broom burgeoning on its shallow embankment before marshland, harbouring shellduck, occurs. Clunes is the first exchange point for the automated Radio Electronic Token Block system which governs train movements north of Inverness.

Originally the viaduct at Beauly was of timber construction. It was replaced early in the 20th century by a steel girder bridge fabricated in Motherwell. In common with the Mersey, the River Beauly doesn't have a source of its own, being born instead of the confluence of the rivers Farrar and Glass near Erchless Castle, some fifteen miles to the west. BEAULY was another station abandoned in 1960, despite serving a community of some significance and tourist appeal. Happily the Highland Rail Partnership brought about its re-opening in 2002, albeit with a short platform which demands that only the central doors on the train are operated by the guard. The brevity of the platform reflects the experimental nature of the re-opening, and doubts in some quarters that the station would attract sufficient use to warrant much expenditure on it. Initial patterns of use suggest such concerns were unduly pessimistic, over sixty passengers per day regularly being recorded as using the station.

**Clachnaharry Swing-bridge**
*Main picture:* a tall-masted vessel makes its way along the Caledonian Canal. *Inset:* returning the bridge to rail use.

'**C**HANGE here for the Black Isle Line', was the running-in board which greeted passengers at MUIR OF ORD for many years. The branch to Fortrose opened in 1894, by all accounts a charming line which wended its thirteen-mile course through fertile farmland, down to its foreshortened terminus on the Moray Firth; for originally it was intended to reach Rosemarkie, a mile further on. By branchline standards it enjoyed a variety of motive power, including a 4-4-0 tank design built by Dubs & Co of Glasgow and originally destined for use in Uruguay. Peter Drummond's handsome 'Small Bens' were another regularly performing class on the line which closed to passenger services in 1951, and goods nine years later.

Muir of Ord was initially a victim of the 1960 sweeping closure programme, but re-opened by public demand in 1976. Just as well, because when the Far North and Kyle lines were temporarily divorced from the rest of the railway system in 1989, following collapse of the Ness Viaduct, Muir of Ord became the southern terminus of operation. A depot was purloined from Barassie - surplus to requirements following completion of the Ayrshire electrification scheme - and erected for rolling stock maintenance. It remains on site today, incongruous in disuse, waiting, perhaps to be whisked away to the scene of some new emergency.

The train climbs away from Muir of Ord for a mile or two before beginning to descend into the valley of the River Conon. Hugh Miller, the Cromarty geologist and thinker, worked as an apprentice mason on the farm adjoining Conon House, a late 18th century mansion in a parkland setting to the west of the line. CONON station was another victim of the 1960 closures, but, buoyed by the success of Beauly, it is being considered as a candidate for re-opening by the ebullient Highland Rail Partnership. Conon might well have become a junction for a branch promoted along the north side of the Black Isle early in the 20th century. It was to have linked the small town of Cromarty with the outside world, and, indeed, a handful of miles of track were laid at the Cromarty end before the Great War intervened and creativity turned - perhaps of necessity, perhaps not - to destruction. Not without irony, the rails were taken up and re-used by the military

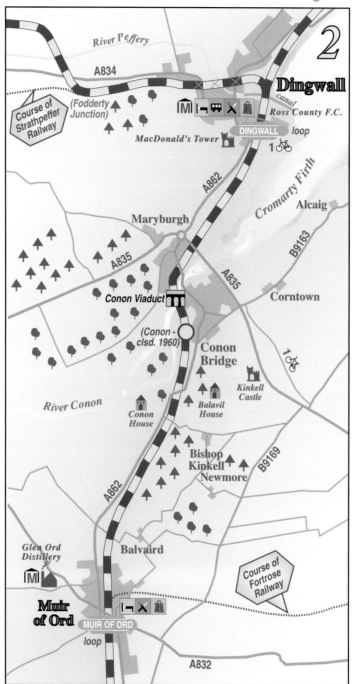

authorities in the Orkneys.

Thomas Telford built a bridge across the Conon in 1809. His typically graceful bridge has been replaced by a modern structure, but it is interesting to note that the toll house remains and is the work of Telford's assistant, Joseph Mitchell, who returned to Conon Bridge some thirty years later as the more celebrated railway engineer responsible for the five arch railway bridge built for the Inverness & Ross-shire Railway in 1862.

A hillside tower overlooks the railway's entry into DINGWALL. It was erected to the memory of Major-General Sir Hector MacDonald, a local hero if ever there was one. The tower was opened in 1907, four years after its subject's suicide in a Paris hotel. 'Fighting Mac', as he was fondly known, was born in humble circumstances on the Black Isle and had risen through the ranks, forging a glittering career in the army which culminated in the Battle of Ombdurman, where he was largely responsible for the victory which avenged Gordon's death in Khartoum. In 1903, whilst in command of the British Forces on the island of Ceylon, rumours circulated questioning the polarity of his sexuality. In point of fact he was a married man with a son, but this had been kept secret because Kitchener frowned upon his senior officers marrying. Sir Hector returned to London to seek King Edward VII's help in clearing his name, but was rebutted. Making his way back to Ceylon to face the music, he came down to breakfast in Paris to see that the affair had become headline news. Quietly putting down the paper, he returned to his bedroom and put a revolver to his head. The accusations brought against him were never proven, and there are suggestions that he was the victim of intrigue and jealousy.

A plaque on Dingwall station records that 134,864 servicemen were given a cup of tea here during the First World War, a statistic reinforcing just how busy the Far North and Kyle lines were, not only during the *war to end all wars* but the subsequent replay as well. In both conflicts the regions north and west of Inverness were restricted zones of paramount military importance and the railways bore the brunt of transport requirements to an extent which is hard to grasp in our road dominated era.

Out through the Booking Hall, on the roadway side of the station, a more sobering reminder of the First World

War can be found in the shape of the Cambrai Memorial, an intensely moving rustic cross erected initially on the battlefield in France in November 1917. The cross was brought back to Dingwall in 1924 by the Seaforth Reunion Club. You can't go far in Scotland without stumbling upon memorials to the dead of both world wars, for by proportion the mortality toll had great impact on life in these sparsely populated areas. An adjacent memorial remembers one John Meikill of Nitshill in Dumfriesshire, killed on 20th July 1918.

Nowadays Dingwall is the only staffed station north of Inverness except for the respective termini at Thurso, Wick and Kyle of Lochalsh. It remains a thoroughly well -appointed station, handsomely constructed in a pinkish sandstone with crow-stepped gables and a fine and airy canopy. A privately-owned and discreetly demure tearoom flourishes in what was once part of the Ladies Waiting Room, and on warm days its tables have a habit of spilling out on to the down platform in a manner reminiscent of Lady Foley's at Malvern. At the other end of the platform, a perhaps more egalitarian in outlook bar also does a roaring trade. It is called 'The Mallard' after the world speed record holding steam locomotive which, as every schoolboy *used* to know, attained a never beaten speed of 126mph between Grantham and Peterborough on a test run in 1938.

Before leaving Dingwall, the driver of your train must leave his cab and set the junction point for the Far North or Kyle route as appropriate. Naturally, in the old days, this would have been the signalman's responsibility. On your right look out for Ross County's football stadium, the most northerly league ground in Great Britain, where, if the football's not going according to plan, at least the pies are brilliant.

Most pub quiz experts would answer the Caledonian Canal if asked to name Britain's most northerly inland waterway, but technically they'd be mistaken, for just over a mile of the River Peffery was canalised in 1817 and the resultant Dingwall Canal quietly flourished for three-quarters of a century before being made redundant by the railway. Oh, and incidentally, it is interesting to note that if you're booking a ticket with Virgin Trains over the telephone, the chances are you'll be dealing with a call centre in Dingwall!

**Saturday Lunch** - on Dingwall's spacious platform

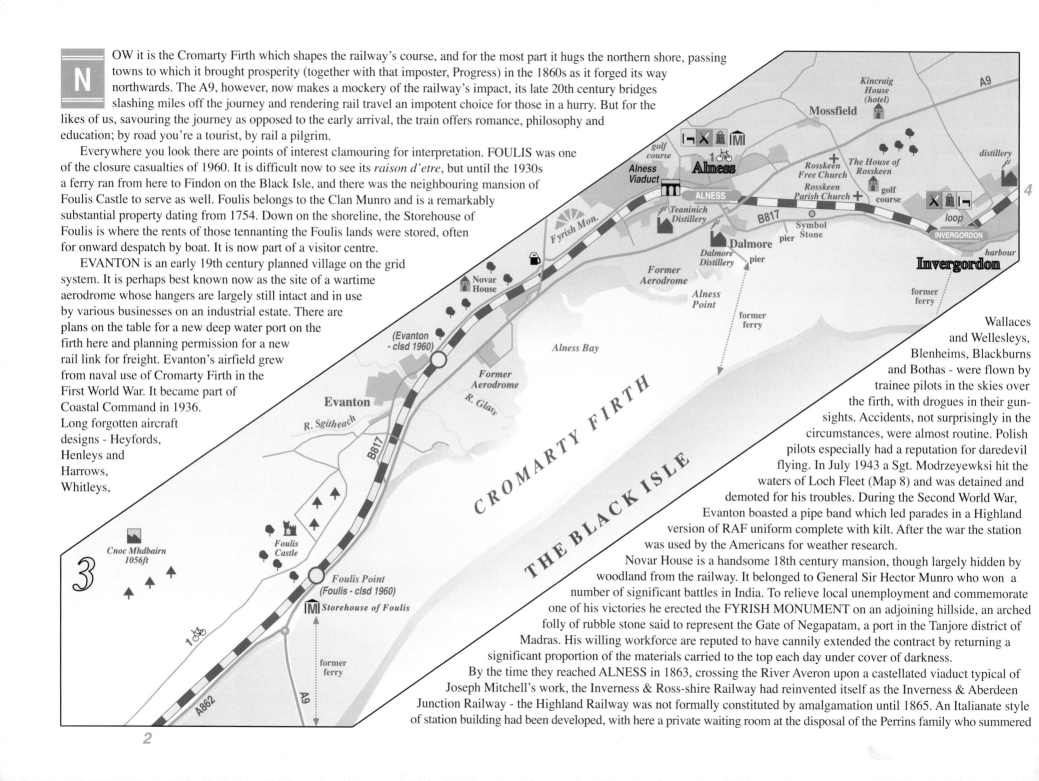

**N**OW it is the Cromarty Firth which shapes the railway's course, and for the most part it hugs the northern shore, passing towns to which it brought prosperity (together with that imposter, Progress) in the 1860s as it forged its way northwards. The A9, however, now makes a mockery of the railway's impact, its late 20th century bridges slashing miles off the journey and rendering rail travel an impotent choice for those in a hurry. But for the likes of us, savouring the journey as opposed to the early arrival, the train offers romance, philosophy and education; by road you're a tourist, by rail a pilgrim.

Everywhere you look there are points of interest clamouring for interpretation. FOULIS was one of the closure casualties of 1960. It is difficult now to see its *raison d'etre*, but until the 1930s a ferry ran from here to Findon on the Black Isle, and there was the neighbouring mansion of Foulis Castle to serve as well. Foulis belongs to the Clan Munro and is a remarkably substantial property dating from 1754. Down on the shoreline, the Storehouse of Foulis is where the rents of those tennanting the Foulis lands were stored, often for onward despatch by boat. It is now part of a visitor centre.

EVANTON is an early 19th century planned village on the grid system. It is perhaps best known now as the site of a wartime aerodrome whose hangers are largely still intact and in use by various businesses on an industrial estate. There are plans on the table for a new deep water port on the firth here and planning permission for a new rail link for freight. Evanton's airfield grew from naval use of Cromarty Firth in the First World War. It became part of Coastal Command in 1936. Long forgotten aircraft designs - Heyfords, Henleys and Harrows, Whitleys,

Wallaces and Wellesleys, Blenheims, Blackburns and Bothas - were flown by trainee pilots in the skies over the firth, with drogues in their gun-sights. Accidents, not surprisingly in the circumstances, were almost routine. Polish pilots especially had a reputation for daredevil flying. In July 1943 a Sgt. Modrzeyewksi hit the waters of Loch Fleet (Map 8) and was detained and demoted for his troubles. During the Second World War, Evanton boasted a pipe band which led parades in a Highland version of RAF uniform complete with kilt. After the war the station was used by the Americans for weather research.

Novar House is a handsome 18th century mansion, though largely hidden by woodland from the railway. It belonged to General Sir Hector Munro who won a number of significant battles in India. To relieve local unemployment and commemorate one of his victories he erected the FYRISH MONUMENT on an adjoining hillside, an arched folly of rubble stone said to represent the Gate of Negapatam, a port in the Tanjore district of Madras. His willing workforce are reputed to have cannily extended the contract by returning a significant proportion of the materials carried to the top each day under cover of darkness.

By the time they reached ALNESS in 1863, crossing the River Averon upon a castellated viaduct typical of Joseph Mitchell's work, the Inverness & Ross-shire Railway had reinvented itself as the Inverness & Aberdeen Junction Railway - the Highland Railway was not formally constituted by amalgamation until 1865. An Italianate style of station building had been developed, with here a private waiting room at the disposal of the Perrins family who summered at Ardross Castle five miles to the north. The family were one half of the Lea & Perrins partnership famous as manufacturers of Worcestershire Sauce. Unfortunately, Alness station (closed in 1960 but re-opened as a result of the oil boom in 1973) was burnt down by vandals and has been replaced by a small functional shelter which hardly does the busy little town on its doorstep justice. In the past the town's two distilleries would have been rail served. The Munro family opened Teaninich Distillery in 1817. Dalmore was founded by Alexander Matheson in 1839. During the First World War it was commandeered to make mines instead of whisky. Many of the casings were brought by train from Kyle of Lochalsh.

It is oil rigs, awaiting maintenance or simply out of use, and the occasional cruise liner, that are seen through the carriage window these days, but once upon a time Cromarty Firth played host to the Home Fleet. If you can bear to look inland, however, try and catch a glimpse of the Parish Church of Rosskeen. The building itself is disused now, but the cemetery remains in use. Amongst its stones are a row of plain servicemen's graves, all recorded as having met their maker aboard HMS *Natal* on 30th December, 1915. A Christmas party was being held on the 13,500 ton cruiser for local civilians and their children when the ship exploded without warning. Over four hundred died as the vessel sank quickly at its moorings. Four years of official secrecy followed before it was revealed that the tragedy was probably caused by an internal explosion in the ships armoury. 1915 was a fraught year on Cromarty Firth. That October, gunners believing themselves under attack from a German submarine, wildly opened fire, shelling the Black Isle village of Jemimaville, causing damage to several houses and injuring a baby. The enemy submarine, it transpired, was probably a seal.

children'. The Invergordon Mutiny lasted two days. The Admiralty climbed down, imposing a more conciliatory cut of 10%.

Invergordon was also a busy base for flying-boats and seaplanes, notably the famous Catalinas and Sunderlands. It was aboard a Sunderland that the Duke of Kent left here on 25th August 1942, bound on an ambassadorial mission to Iceland. Despite low cloud conditions, it should have been a routine flight for the Duke, fourth in line to the throne, but half an hour after taking off from the Cromarty Firth the flying-boat mysteriously veered off course and crashed into a hillside near Dunbeath, north of Helmsdale. Fourteen of the fifteen men on board were killed, but a wireless operator, flying in the rear turret, survived. Conspiracy theories abound as to the reason for the crash, and the flying-boat's sudden deviation from its north-easterly course. But they often do in such circumstances, and it seems likely that an error in the operation of a newly installed compass, together with the cloudy conditions, is the most likely, if mundane, explanation. The RAF bases at Invergordon and Alness closed in 1946, but there are still tangible remains and memorials to be seen in the vicinity.

Oil rigs under repair loom over the skeletal remnants of INVERGORDON station. It must have once been an impressive stop on the Far North line. You can sense that from the

Ignore for a moment the rather ugly oil rigs. Picture in their place battleships, aircraft-carriers, cruisers and destroyers. In September 1931 the Navy announced pay reductions throughout the ranks in the order of 25%. At that time an Admiral's pay was eight pounds per day, an able seaman's four shillings. The smaller the pocket, the harder the cut in income. The Atlantic Fleet was due out on manoeuvres, but the ratings on the battleships *Valiant* and *Rodney* refused to leave their quarters. One sailor told the press: 'We don't want any Bolshevik stuff. We are not disloyal. We don't mind giving something up but we cannot have the Admiralty taking a shilling off our pay. This is not sacrifice, it is starvation of our wives and

defenestrated Jacobean entrance on the up platform, and from the elegant cast-iron bracketing which continues to support the canopy. You can choose between watching ant-like figures at work high up on the rigs, or the more leisurely activity of bowls on a rink beside the station while waiting for the next train. To give Invergordon's economy a boost after the Royal Navy had departed, an aluminium smelter was established at the edge of the town in 1968. But this new activity failed to sustain itself and closed a decade later. A blending and bottling distillery, together with an industrial estate, provide additional employment to the oil rig maintenance yards now.

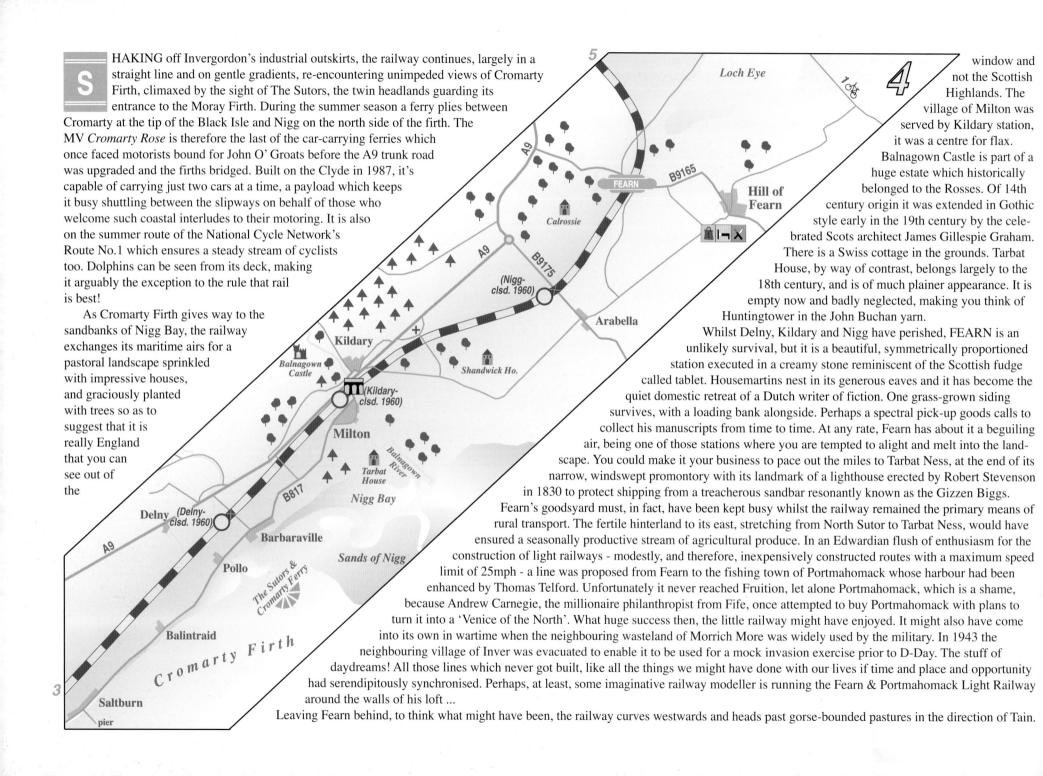

**S**HAKING off Invergordon's industrial outskirts, the railway continues, largely in a straight line and on gentle gradients, re-encountering unimpeded views of Cromarty Firth, climaxed by the sight of The Sutors, the twin headlands guarding its entrance to the Moray Firth. During the summer season a ferry plies between Cromarty at the tip of the Black Isle and Nigg on the north side of the firth. The MV *Cromarty Rose* is therefore the last of the car-carrying ferries which once faced motorists bound for John O' Groats before the A9 trunk road was upgraded and the firths bridged. Built on the Clyde in 1987, it's capable of carrying just two cars at a time, a payload which keeps it busy shuttling between the slipways on behalf of those who welcome such coastal interludes to their motoring. It is also on the summer route of the National Cycle Network's Route No.1 which ensures a steady stream of cyclists too. Dolphins can be seen from its deck, making it arguably the exception to the rule that rail is best!

As Cromarty Firth gives way to the sandbanks of Nigg Bay, the railway exchanges its maritime airs for a pastoral landscape sprinkled with impressive houses, and graciously planted with trees so as to suggest that it is really England that you can see out of the window and not the Scottish Highlands. The village of Milton was served by Kildary station, it was a centre for flax. Balnagown Castle is part of a huge estate which historically belonged to the Rosses. Of 14th century origin it was extended in Gothic style early in the 19th century by the celebrated Scots architect James Gillespie Graham. There is a Swiss cottage in the grounds. Tarbat House, by way of contrast, belongs largely to the 18th century, and is of much plainer appearance. It is empty now and badly neglected, making you think of Huntingtower in the John Buchan yarn.

Whilst Delny, Kildary and Nigg have perished, FEARN is an unlikely survival, but it is a beautiful, symmetrically proportioned station executed in a creamy stone reminiscent of the Scottish fudge called tablet. Housemartins nest in its generous eaves and it has become the quiet domestic retreat of a Dutch writer of fiction. One grass-grown siding survives, with a loading bank alongside. Perhaps a spectral pick-up goods calls to collect his manuscripts from time to time. At any rate, Fearn has about it a beguiling air, being one of those stations where you are tempted to alight and melt into the landscape. You could make it your business to pace out the miles to Tarbat Ness, at the end of its narrow, windswept promontory with its landmark of a lighthouse erected by Robert Stevenson in 1830 to protect shipping from a treacherous sandbar resonantly known as the Gizzen Biggs.

Fearn's goodsyard must, in fact, have been kept busy whilst the railway remained the primary means of rural transport. The fertile hinterland to its east, stretching from North Sutor to Tarbat Ness, would have ensured a seasonally productive stream of agricultural produce. In an Edwardian flush of enthusiasm for the construction of light railways - modestly, and therefore, inexpensively constructed routes with a maximum speed limit of 25mph - a line was proposed from Fearn to the fishing town of Portmahomack whose harbour had been enhanced by Thomas Telford. Unfortunately it never reached Fruition, let alone Portmahomack, which is a shame, because Andrew Carnegie, the millionaire philanthropist from Fife, once attempted to buy Portmahomack with plans to turn it into a 'Venice of the North'. What huge success then, the little railway might have enjoyed. It might also have come into its own in wartime when the neighbouring wasteland of Morrich More was widely used by the military. In 1943 the neighbouring village of Inver was evacuated to enable it to be used for a mock invasion exercise prior to D-Day. The stuff of daydreams! All those lines which never got built, like all the things we might have done with our lives if time and place and opportunity had serendipitously synchronised. Perhaps, at least, some imaginative railway modeller is running the Fearn & Portmahomack Light Railway around the walls of his loft ...

Leaving Fearn behind, to think what might have been, the railway curves westwards and heads past gorse-bounded pastures in the direction of Tain.

The Farmlands of Fearn - *Main picture:* Inverness bound train near Calrossie. *Inset:* the handsome symmetry of Fearn station.

**O** LD photographs reveal that the first thing passengers from the south would see on entering TAIN (apart from the ruined 13th century chapel dedicated to St Duthac) was a neat little two-road engine shed built of stone. In the British Railways era this was coded 60C, a sub-shed of Helmsdale. There's a nice picture of it in Peter Tatlow's *Highland Miscellany* (OPC, 1985) in LMS days with *Ben Alisky* simmering contentedly outside. In the final years of the depot's use, a Caledonian 4-4-0 was its sole inhabitant. Tain station, opened in 1864, has a well-proportioned air about it, a quiet confidence in its place in the community. Its Grade II listing reflects its status, but whilst it has unfortunately been empty for a number of years, there's a strong possibility that it may soon be taken up as a base for rail maintenance engineers. Low-lying on the edge of the Dornoch Firth, fears that it might be prone to flooding have deterred those seeking a more dynamic use for this handsome building. A commuter train leaves Tain each morning calling at stations to Inverness, exactly an hour away, half the time that the first up train of the day took in 1950!

During your brief stay at Tain station - brief, that is, if you are not waiting to pass a late-running service in the opposite direction - you can peer through the carriage window at this pleasant little town's elegantly towered and turreted skyline, and grapple with the urge to alight. Even a pyrrhic victory in this respect will have its compensations, for north of Tain the line embarks upon yet another highly scenic section of the journey. One mile and 13 chains north of Tain the line passes one of Scotland's best known distilleries. Like many whisky makers, Glenmorangie were boosted by the advent of the railway and relied upon its transport links for over a hundred years. Doubtless, that old Caley 4-4-0, sub-shedded at Tain, would have loped up the line most mornings of the week, bringing peat and barley in for the distillery and taking its finished nectar out. Glenmorangie Siding closed in June, 1970. It is bewilderingly frustrating that the whisky industry, throughout Scotland makes such little use of rail freight; but, in truth, such traffics were largely driven away by British Rail's indifference in an era when the diminishing number of freight trains being operated at all were widely perceived as running to make life easy for the railway rather than the customer, a sorry state of affairs which HRP and EWS, amongst others, are actively attempting to reverse.

Dornoch Firth comes back into focus, exposing a lumpy foreshore of gleaming mud at low tide.

In clear conditions the northern horizon can offer glimpses as far as the sugar-loaf-shaped summit of Morven in Caithness, thirty miles away, which dominates the penultimate section of the journey down to Georgemas Junction; (Maps 13/14). In the middle distance, yet still the best part of an hour away by train, the 1st Duke of Sutherland's monument stands on a hillside overlooking Golspie (Map 9). Nearer at hand stands Ben Tarvie's unmistakably whale-like outline - you will see its reverse image as the train descends through Strath Fleet (Map 8) in due course.

The railway's capacity to reintroduce you to different angles of the same view - as a composer might create variations on a musical theme - might have been diluted had proposals (in the middle of the nineteen-eighties) to redirect it beside the new Dornoch Firth Road Bridge been adopted. At the time railway campaigners felt cheated that the reasonably cost-effective opportunity to provide the new two-lane bridge with a parallel structure carrying a single railway track was not seized upon. Not only would construction of a new line cut over twenty miles off the journey, it would have restored railway services to Dornoch, the most tourist-significant centre in the area. Such improvements, however, would have occurred at the expense of the railway's huge inland curve via the Kyles of Shin, Lairg and Strath Fleet, and that would

**5**

Spinningdale
A949
*ruined mill*
Newton Point
Hut Circle
Burial Mound
Ardmore Point
*Struie Hill 1082ft*
Ardmore
golf course
Former Meikle Ferry
Balblair Distillery
(Edderton-clsd 1960)
Symbol Stone
**Edderton**
*Cambuscurrie Bay*
*Edderton Sands*
Edderton (Meikle Ferry-clsd 1869)
A836
Cuthill Sands
Dornoch Firth Bridge
*Ben Tarvie Beinn a' Bhragaidh Morven etc.*
Ardjachie Point
*Dornoch Sands*
*D o r n o c h   F i r t h*
*Glenmorangie Distillery*
A9
A9
**Tain**
TAIN
loop
golf course
remains of St Duthac's Chapel
*River Tain*

**6**

**4**

socially, let alone scenically, have been a huge sacrifice.

The Queen Mother opened the 890 metres long Dornoch Firth Bridge in 1991. Prior to that, motorists also had to bear inland, as far as Bonar Bridge. The Meikle Ferry had ceased operating formally in 1957. It had been an ancient means of crossing the mile-wide firth. When the railway reached here in 1864, a temporary terminus was provided, with horse-drawn connections via the ferry to Dornoch and the north. But four months later the line had proceeded to Bonar Bridge, where there was already a Telford-built bridge across the much narrower Kyle of Sutherland, a more reliable route to the north. Rendered largely obsolete, MEIKLE FERRY station closed five years after being opened, though, remarkably, the station building remains intact and in use as an inn - in the midst of a caravan site!

Fifty-five years before the railway arrived, on Wednesday 16th August, 1809, a large party bound, in high spirits, for the Lammas Fair at Tain, boarded the ferry on the Dornoch side, unheeding suggestions that the vessel was overloaded. After rowing out from the shore, then hoisting the sail, water began shipping over the gunwales. The ferrymen turned back, but the boat sank before it could reach shallow water. Ninety-nine people drowned. There were just a dozen survivors. Joseph Mitchell's father, John, an associate of Thomas Telford's, had a narrow escape. He had arrived too late to catch the ferry, and could only watch helplessly from the shore as the disaster unfolded. A contemporary list of the dead, reproduced in Dornoch's excellent Historylinks museum, makes sober reading: sisters and servants, soldiers and shoemakers, along with the two ferrymen themselves - Donald Chisholm and William Sutherland. There were still Sutherlands operating the ferry when it closed a century and a half later. In 1831 Robert Stevenson considered erecting of a wooden bridge at the narrowest part of the firth between Ardmore Point and Newton Point, but travellers had to wait for the Queen Mother's opening ceremony before the firth became truly irrelevant to travellers north and south.

EDDERTON station closed in 1960, but the building remains in domestic use, its occupants rather enviously located alongside a distillery. Balblair's single malt is not perhaps so widely promoted as its counterpart along the line at Glenmorangie, but it can similarly trace its origins back to the 18th century. The present distillery dates from 1895, being re-sited to take advantage of rail transport. Its peaty water supply runs off Struie Hill. See-sawing along a sequence of untaxing gradients the railway continues its way beside the narrowing firth. Across the water you might just see the ruin of a five-storey cotton mill at Spinningdale. Constructed in 1793 to bring work to a largely destitute area, it failed because, like many Highland initiatives, before and since, it was too far from its potential markets. It was damaged by fire in 1806 and never repaired.

Karen Tanguy

**Whisky Country**
*Main picture:* Balblair Distillery, Edderton.
*Inset:* Glenmorangie Distillery, Tain.

**B**ETWEEN the Easter and Wester Fearn burns the railway launches out on a causeway across a bay in the firth, so that for a moment, whichever way you look from the train, you are under the illusion that it has become a hydrofoil, skimming low across the water. Reality returns with views of the huge bowed bridge at Bonar Bridge. Dating from 1973, it is the third bridge on the site, following Telford's 1812 'overture' and its 1893 replacement. Mid Fearn station remained in the public timetable for just eleven months, thereafter remaining an unadvertised stop for the inhabitants of Fearn Lodge. The station at ARDGAY (pronounced Ard-guy) was known, until 1977, as Bonar Bridge, it marked the terminus of the Inverness & Aberdeen Junction Railway and opened for business on the 1st October, 1864. Both the station building and the stationmaster's house remain in domestic use, the former jocularly known as 'Loco Cottage'. As a whole the station wears a gloomy air, but you can peep through the trees bordering the up platform to picturesque expanses of the firth beyond.

So, after the train pulls away from Ardgay, you are embarking upon a route built by another independent company, the Sutherland Railway, incorporated under an Act of Parliament in 1865, with powers to build a railway to Brora, almost thirty-three miles away. By then the Highland Railway had been formed and they invested in the scheme, but that did not prevent it from running short of capital on a number of occasions, for there were viaducts to build over the River Carron and the Kyle of Shin, and a considerable amount of rock-blasting required on the climb to Lairg. Carron Viaduct is a comparatively modest double-arch masonry affair, but the Shin (or Oykel) Viaduct which spans the Kyle of Sutherland, and which marks the old boundary between that county and Ross-shire, is a marvellous structure, jointly attributed to Joseph Mitchell and Murdoch Paterson. The main, iron-truss span is 230 feet in length, whilst on either side are masonry approach arches. Initially there was only to be a station on the north bank of the kyle at INVERSHIN, but presumably the grandees of Culrain Lodge felt disenfranchised, and subsequently a platform opened at CULRAIN, less than half a mile away. The fare between the two stations in Highland Railway days was just a ha'penny. Nowadays it's 90p, but a rare transaction since a pedestrian footbridge was added to the viaduct in 2000.

In a reverse of past significance, one might argue that Invershin could close. Culrain remains busy with back-packers overnighting in the grandiose Youth Hostel located in Carbisdale Castle, but Invershin is hardly used. Carbisdale Castle was built in 1911 for Duchess Blair, widow of the 3rd Duke of Sutherland, who did so much to promote and fund the railway to the Far North. Carbisdale, constructed on the estate of the subsequently demolished Culrain Lodge, acquired the sobriquet 'Castle Spite'. After being his mistress, Mary Blair had been the Duke's second wife and was ostracised by his heirs. Litigation surrounded the contents of the Duke's will. At one point the Duchess had infamously seized a letter from under the very noses of a group of lawyers and flung it on the fire. A letter, it was conjectured, which might have thrown light on whether the Duke had been implicated in the mysterious death of her former husband. She was briefly gaoled in Holloway Prison for her troubles! Banned from living in Dunrobin Castle (Map 9), and, indeed, anywhere in Sutherland, following a short-lived marriage to the wealthy MP Sir Albert Rollit, Mary Blair purchased the Culrain estate and proceeded to erect this vast and elaborate house: whether

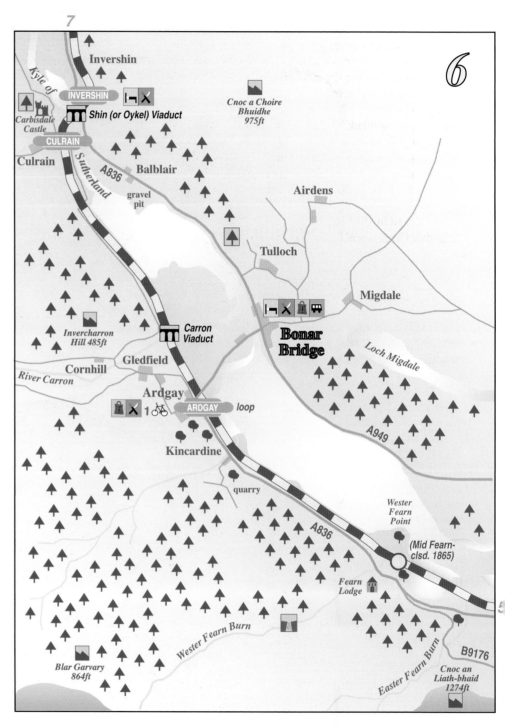

to cock a snook at her former family-in-law, or out of cherished affection for her second husband, one can only guess. There was no love lost: the Sutherland heirs, passing by train, would make a point of drawing the carriage blinds until the reviled building passed from view; on her instructions, the architects designed a clocktower with only three faces, the fourth, facing Sutherland, being blank, visibly stating that she was not prepared to give them the time of day. Following her death in 1912, it passed to her daughter and then Theodore Salveson, a member of the whaling and shipping dynasty, who harpooned it for the sum of just £1,500 in 1933. During the Second World War it became a bolt hole for members of the Norwegian Resistance, and in 1944 King Haakon VII attended the 'Carbisdale Conference' here, which determined that Norway would make its own future when the war ended, and not be swallowed by the Soviet bloc. Now it is a surreally palatial youth hostel, or in the words of the *Rough Guide to Scotland*: 'one of the most opulent Youth Hostels in the world'.

**Turning Inland -**
Mid-Fearn, Ardgay and Invershin

**Glen Achany Freight** - *Main picture:* the 'Safeway Flyer' climbs up to Lairg. *Inset:* oil being shunted at Lairg.

JUST as the salmon go leaping up the Falls of Shin, so must the train start working hard to climb the 1 in 72 to Lairg. The summit, two miles beyond Lairg (Map 8) is 488 feet above sea level, Invershin a mere 50 feet. Threading its way through Achany's luxuriantly wooded glen, the railway zig-zags with the contours as if wholly organic in origin. Caressed by waving fronds of bracken and fern, you begin to imagine that the train is really perhaps a wild deer being ridden bareback, and not the utilitarian product of a workshop in Derby at all.

Upstream of Invershin is the confluence of the rivers Oykel and Shin. The Oykel's source lies amongst the crags and corries of the Munro, Ben More Assynt, the highest point in Sutherland; the Shin flows out of its eponymous loch, a massive sheet of water, almost twenty miles long, running north-west of Lairg. Hydro-electricity developments came to the River Shin in the 1950s, and there are well environmentally integrated generating stations at Lairg and Shin Bridge. Fascinatingly, though, they were not the first attempts at power generation in the area. After the First World War, Sir William Edgar Horne purchased the Lairg Estate from the 5th Duke of Sutherland, and installed a diesel generator to provide the village with electricity. This was not his only contribution to the local economy. Beside the railway station a brickworks was opened, and nearby a laundry, a sawmill and a dairy. Additionally, he financed construction of the postal sorting office which remains an important cog in the Royal Mail's highland delivery network to this day.

A glimpse through trees reveals the dignified frontage of Achany House which dates from 1810, but which was added to twice during Victoria's reign to designs by the Maitland partnership, an influential family of architects based in Tain.

We aren't the first to find this landscape conducive. The hillsides are peppered with Stone Age remains: burial cairns, hut circles and field systems. On Ord Hill, to the west of Little Loch Shin, an Archaeological Trail has been devised to illustrate differing facets of the life led here two, three and even five thousand years ago. It makes the railway's coming, in 1868,

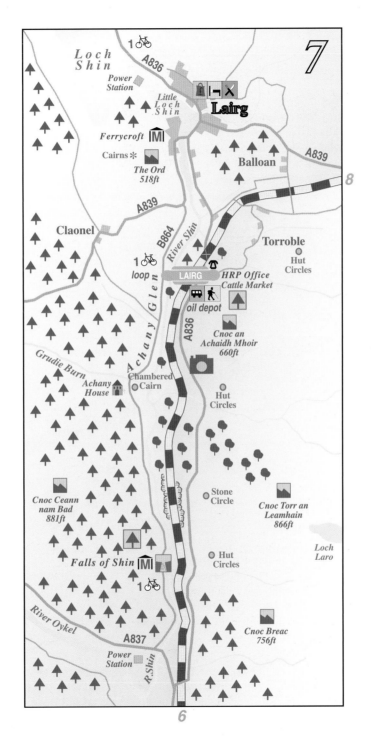

the merest scratch on the Formica top of time.

A mile out of the village, LAIRG station remains a significant transport interchange, an excellent example of how a village railway station might flourish, forward-lookingly, into the 21st century. In typical Sutherland Railway style, the station building on the up platform is self-effacingly vernacular. Misleadingly, it might have been there before the railway, a crofter's cottage or small farmhouse, slate-roofed with dormer windows like eyebrows raised in mild astonishment. For a while after the station became unstaffed it lay empty, but now it houses the offices of the Highland Rail Partnership, a thoroughly appropriate new use. And evidence of how effective the HRP have been is to be seen hard by where the oil depot has recently been re-linked to the rail network, receiving regular deliveries from Grangemouth and thereby keeping significant numbers of tanker lorries off the Highlands' narrow roads. Other transport interfaces include Macleod's bus services, which meet most trains and the Royal Mail's Postbus network which provides connections to the far shores of the West Coast. Sadly, from a spectator's point of view, train-connecting buses no longer go through the time-honoured routine of reversing down a ramp on to the crossing-board in order to make easier work of the laborious process of loading and unloading goods, parcels and even livestock bound for remote country destinations beyond the reach of the railway. There's an evocatively nostalgic picture in Robert Grieves's *Wheels Around Caithness & Sutherland* (Stenlake 2003) of a Sutherland Transport bus going through this very process, taken in the 1960s when buses still connected with the mail trains.

Mention of livestock also recalls an important facet of railway working at Lairg concerning the annual sheep sales. The sales still take place at the auction mart beside the station, but inevitably all the animals travel by road now. The mart was opened by MacDonald Fraser in 1896, and even into the 1950s up to ten special livestock trains would be operated in conjunction with the autumn sales: in August 1959 112 cattle wagons were despatched from Lairg in *one day!* In 1890 construction of a railway from Lairg to Laxford near Cape Wrath was considered. What a nice ride *that* would have been!

FTER heading north through Glen Achany, the railway bears east beyond Lairg Summit and begins a beautiful descent into Strath Fleet. The thing about the Far North line is that it traverses such a variety of landscapes. If Alexander Frater once memorably likened the Kyle of Lochalsh line to a three-movement concerto, then by the same analogy the route between Inverness and Wick and Thurso must be a *tour de force* of epic proportions, the railway equivalent of Rachmaninov's *Rhapsody on a Theme of Paganini* or Elgar's *Enigma Variations*.

Eastbound the summit is breasted at 1 in 70, westbound a marginally gentler 1 in 80. Despite the proximity of the A839 there is a wildness about the summit defined by Scots pine and a large tract of heather. An isolated surfaceman's cottage only serves to emphasise the loneliness of the scene. Down under the heathery flank of Leathad Ghaicarain the line runs accompanied by the River Fleet, little more than a peaty burn at this stage in its career. At Acheilidh there was once a crossing loop, the sort of scene which might have inspired Hamilton Ellis to paint an up Loch-hauled fish extra crossing a down Castle-hauled mail with a buzzard perched on a fence post watching on. Heather gives way to bog and bog to acceptable pastureland, though the valley barely widens. Muie is remembered for its Martyrs who in 1882 defied their landlord's clearance scheme and followed their period of imprisonment with a heroes homecoming. Far further back in time the district was occupied by Norsemen. On the hill above Dalmore there was a quarry linked to the main line by a narrow gauge incline. Also near Dalmore is a lineside cairn marking the site of the former home of the grandparents of Canada's first Prime Minister, Sir John Alexander MacDonald. Sir John was born in Glasgow in 1815 and one might reasonably hazard a guess that his grandparents had been evicted from Strath Fleet. The cairn is built from the rubble of the family home. Sir John died in Ottawa in 1891.

The train crosses the River Fleet and slows for the loop at ROGART, 77 miles from Inverness. Rogart was one of the victims of the sweeping closure programme of 13th June, 1960. Yet someone at head office must have had a conscience, for it re-opened (albeit unstaffed) the following March. Nowadays it has the status of a request stop, though most trains seem to stop, if only to cross an oncoming

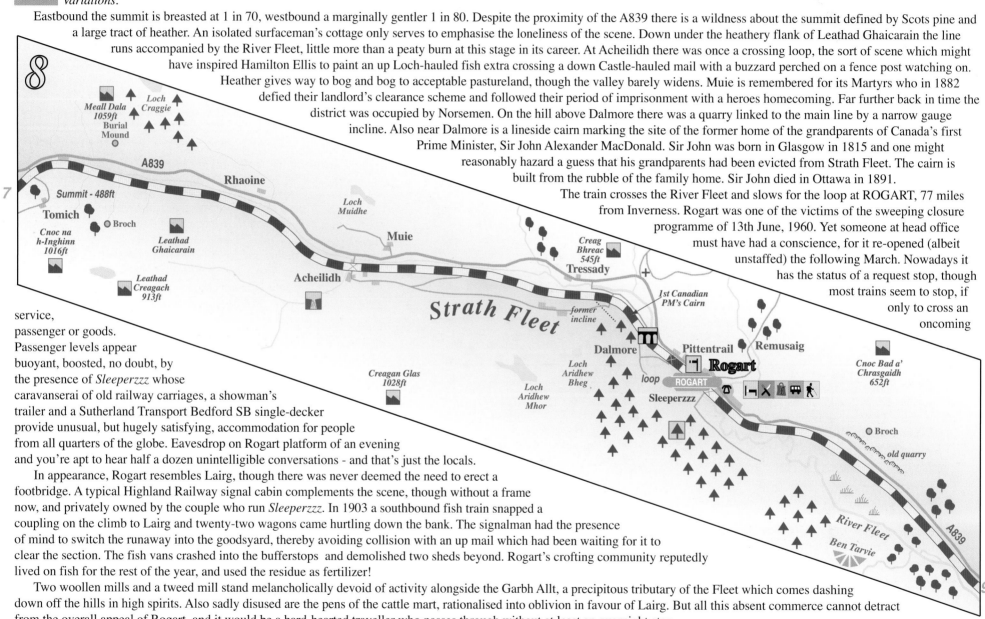

service, passenger or goods. Passenger levels appear buoyant, boosted, no doubt, by the presence of *Sleeperzzz* whose caravanserai of old railway carriages, a showman's trailer and a Sutherland Transport Bedford SB single-decker provide unusual, but hugely satisfying, accommodation for people from all quarters of the globe. Eavesdrop on Rogart platform of an evening and you're apt to hear half a dozen unintelligible conversations - and that's just the locals.

In appearance, Rogart resembles Lairg, though there was never deemed the need to erect a footbridge. A typical Highland Railway signal cabin complements the scene, though without a frame now, and privately owned by the couple who run *Sleeperzzz*. In 1903 a southbound fish train snapped a coupling on the climb to Lairg and twenty-two wagons came hurtling down the bank. The signalman had the presence of mind to switch the runaway into the goodsyard, thereby avoiding collision with an up mail which had been waiting for it to clear the section. The fish vans crashed into the bufferstops and demolished two sheds beyond. Rogart's crofting community reputedly lived on fish for the rest of the year, and used the residue as fertilizer!

Two woollen mills and a tweed mill stand melancholically devoid of activity alongside the Garbh Allt, a precipitous tributary of the Fleet which comes dashing down off the hills in high spirits. Also sadly disused are the pens of the cattle mart, rationalised into oblivion in favour of Lairg. But all this absent commerce cannot detract from the overall appeal of Rogart, and it would be a hard-hearted traveller who passes through without at least an overnight stop.

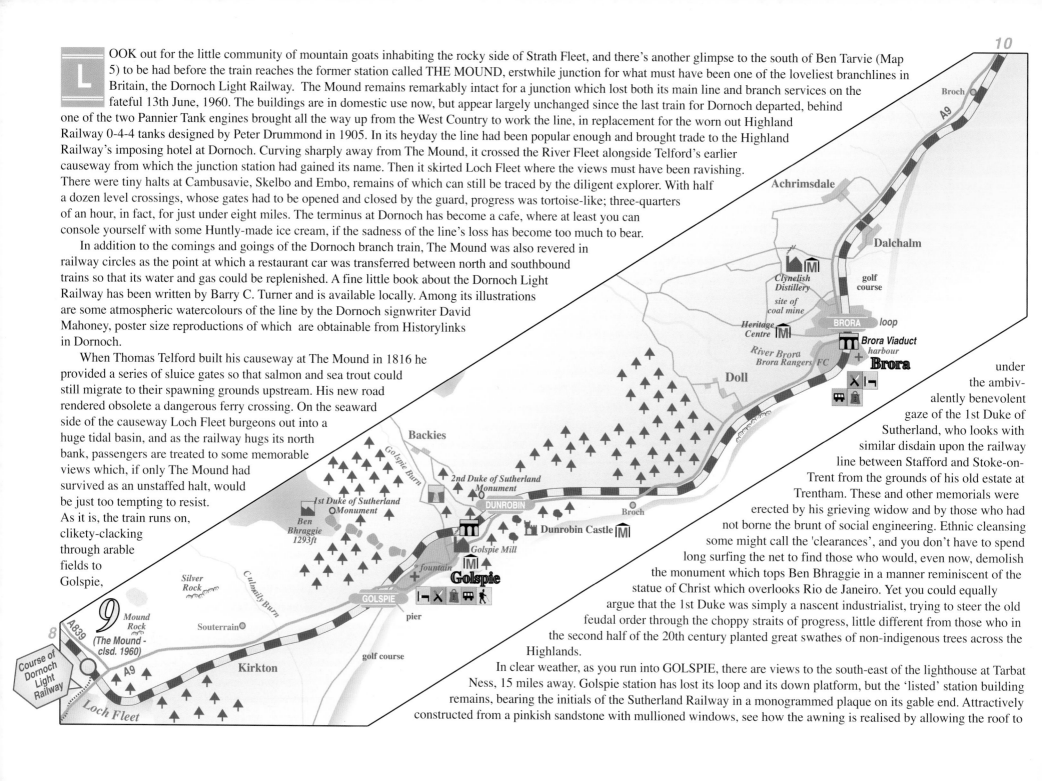

**L**OOK out for the little community of mountain goats inhabiting the rocky side of Strath Fleet, and there's another glimpse to the south of Ben Tarvie (Map 5) to be had before the train reaches the former station called THE MOUND, erstwhile junction for what must have been one of the loveliest branchlines in Britain, the Dornoch Light Railway. The Mound remains remarkably intact for a junction which lost both its main line and branch services on the fateful 13th June, 1960. The buildings are in domestic use now, but appear largely unchanged since the last train for Dornoch departed, behind one of the two Pannier Tank engines brought all the way up from the West Country to work the line, in replacement for the worn out Highland Railway 0-4-4 tanks designed by Peter Drummond in 1905. In its heyday the line had been popular enough and brought trade to the Highland Railway's imposing hotel at Dornoch. Curving sharply away from The Mound, it crossed the River Fleet alongside Telford's earlier causeway from which the junction station had gained its name. Then it skirted Loch Fleet where the views must have been ravishing. There were tiny halts at Cambusavie, Skelbo and Embo, remains of which can still be traced by the diligent explorer. With half a dozen level crossings, whose gates had to be opened and closed by the guard, progress was tortoise-like; three-quarters of an hour, in fact, for just under eight miles. The terminus at Dornoch has become a cafe, where at least you can console yourself with some Huntly-made ice cream, if the sadness of the line's loss has become too much to bear.

In addition to the comings and goings of the Dornoch branch train, The Mound was also revered in railway circles as the point at which a restaurant car was transferred between north and southbound trains so that its water and gas could be replenished. A fine little book about the Dornoch Light Railway has been written by Barry C. Turner and is available locally. Among its illustrations are some atmospheric watercolours of the line by the Dornoch signwriter David Mahoney, poster size reproductions of which are obtainable from Historylinks in Dornoch.

When Thomas Telford built his causeway at The Mound in 1816 he provided a series of sluice gates so that salmon and sea trout could still migrate to their spawning grounds upstream. His new road rendered obsolete a dangerous ferry crossing. On the seaward side of the causeway Loch Fleet burgeons out into a huge tidal basin, and as the railway hugs its north bank, passengers are treated to some memorable views which, if only The Mound had survived as an unstaffed halt, would be just too tempting to resist. As it is, the train runs on, clikety-clacking through arable fields to Golspie,

under the ambivalently benevolent gaze of the 1st Duke of Sutherland, who looks with similar disdain upon the railway line between Stafford and Stoke-on-Trent from the grounds of his old estate at Trentham. These and other memorials were erected by his grieving widow and by those who had not borne the brunt of social engineering. Ethnic cleansing some might call the 'clearances', and you don't have to spend long surfing the net to find those who would, even now, demolish the monument which tops Ben Bhraggie in a manner reminiscent of the statue of Christ which overlooks Rio de Janeiro. Yet you could equally argue that the 1st Duke was simply a nascent industrialist, trying to steer the old feudal order through the choppy straits of progress, little different from those who in the second half of the 20th century planted great swathes of non-indigenous trees across the Highlands.

In clear weather, as you run into GOLSPIE, there are views to the south-east of the lighthouse at Tarbat Ness, 15 miles away. Golspie station has lost its loop and its down platform, but the 'listed' station building remains, bearing the initials of the Sutherland Railway in a monogrammed plaque on its gable end. Attractively constructed from a pinkish sandstone with mullioned windows, see how the awning is realised by allowing the roof to overhang at a different pitch. It is attributed to William Fowler who designed many buildings on the Sutherland Estates from 1857 onwards. The roadbridge at the north end of the platform carries a plaque commemorating the 3rd Duke's 'patriotic zeal and munificence' in developing the railway to the North and 'bringing new industry to the region'. A timber goods shed, of typical Highland Railway design, stands in the trackless goodsyard.

The Sutherland Railway had powers to build to Brora but ran out of money and momentum. In his enthusiasm for railways, the 3rd Duke (who had spent some time learning engineering at the London & North Western Railway works at Wolverton in Buckinghamshire) stepped in and promoted his own railway to Helmsdale. This was a man in love with machinery who had sailed on the sea trials of Brunel's *Great Eastern*. You will encounter further evidence of his passion just along the line. Meanwhile the train faces a steep climb of 1 in 60 out of Golspie, skirting the back of this linear town and affording a glimpse of an ornate Memorial Fountain designed by Sir Charles Barry (of Houses of Parliament fame) in memory of the Duchess of Sutherland - the lady, that is, not the steam locomotive. A high, single arch bridge by Murdoch Paterson carries the line over Golspie Burn, the waters of which tumble down the glen to provide power for Golspie Mill whose oatmeal can be purchased locally.

You have grown accustomed to the Far North route's station architecture, but nothing prepares you for DUNROBIN CASTLE, an astonishing black and white confection of half-timbering, lovingly maintained by the Small Stations Society, who lease it from the present Duchess of Sutherland on peppercorn terms. Rebuilt in its present rustic style in 1902 - and sharing with Falls of Cruachan on the Oban line the distinction of only appearing in the summer timetable - it contains a delightful exhibition of railwayana which opens to the public when excursion trains arrive, as they do on three or four occasions each year. At other times access for groups can be arranged with the Small Stations Society - see Information.

Secretly ensconced within a nondescript shed on the platform is a little petrol driven miniature railway locomotive called Brora. It was built by Baguleys of Burton-on-Trent in 1930 and worked in the grounds of Trentham Gardens for many years. Dunrobin Castle, Sir Charles Barry's not un-Disney-like seat of the Sutherlands, stands at the end of an avenue leading down from the station, a landmark for miles along the coast.

A more modest statue of the 2nd Duke of Sutherland - when compared to that of his father - overlooks the little station. In the absence of a statue to the 3rd Duke, one might say that the railway is *his* memorial. At Dunrobin he had his own engine shed which housed a 2-4-0 tank engine called *Dunrobin* which the Duke was entitled to drive, for after all he had *paid* for the railway! A navvy told to a reporter from *The Times*: 'That's what I call a real duke; driving his own engine, on his own railway, and burning his own blessed coals!'; the latter being a witty reference to that fact that the Duke also owned the coal mine at Brora, as we shall see. The Sutherland's retained the right to drive over their own railway up to Nationalisation in 1948, and also to couple their private carriage to the overnight sleeper to London. The 4th Duke ordered a 0-4-4 replacement for Dunrobin from Sharp Stewart in 1895 and bestowed upon it the same name. After being purchased by Captain Howey of Romney, Hythe & Dymchurch Railway fame, the second *Dunrobin* ended up in a museum in British Columbia from where, who knows, it may return one day. The family's sumptuous private carriage resides in the National Railway Museum in York.

The line departs from Dunrobin as steeply as it arrived, being built across a shallow headland so as not to invade the privacy of the castle and its grounds. A well preserved broch stands beside the line where it is crossed by the A9. Brochs are double-skinned towers dating from between 100BC and 100AD. They may have originally been as tall as thirty or forty feet and were used as defensive farmsteads. Defensive remains of a much later era also abound on the coastline up to Helmsdale. They date from the Second World War and were used as listening posts before radar came into its own. Will they be as enigmatically mysterious in the fourth millennium as the broch is to us now?

You can sow all the industrial acorn seeds you like, but there's no guarantee of riches here in the Highlands. Hunters lineside tweed and knitwear works closed down in Brora in 2003. The Dukes of Sutherland were likewise habitual bedfellows of economic disappointment. The sheep that the 1st Duke introduced following the clearances were not to prove notably viable; the sea fishing he had hoped that those evicted from their homes would engage in, similarly so. The 3rd Duke attempted to get oil out of the peat, opened an ironworks and a brickworks in Brora, and must have believed that his boat had come in with the Kildonan gold rush (Map 10). His coal mines in North Staffordshire were far more productive than his coal mine in Brora which opened in 1873, though coal had been dug in the area since the 16th century. Yet, although coal mining in Brora was never an easy business to be in, its somehow survived as an industrial activity until as recently as 1974, and was even known for a while in the 1950s as the National Coal Board's most northerly pit.

Talking of being northernmost, only Wick Academy prevent Brora Rangers from laying claim to being the most northerly football club on the Scottish mainland. They play in the Highland League, were founded in 1878, and are nicknamed 'The Cattachs'. Brora's ground is called Dudgen Park and you catch a glimpse of it as you approach from the south.

A broad-arched viaduct carries the train across the River Brora into BRORA station. Glance down at the picturesque harbour and the river's sandy entrance to the sea, and try and get a glimpse of the turf-covered ice house, a feature of these little ports given the need to prolong the freshness of a catch if it were to be profitably exported beyond the local market. Coal, bricks, fish - Brora's goodsyard must have been a hectic location in the old days. The goods shed survives, an interesting addendum to a deplorably dilapidated station building, too frequently the subject of vandalism for any sustainable use to be made of it.

From being on the cliff tops south of Brora, the railway descends almost to sea level. Look inland for a moment and you'll see some interesting summits - Cnoc Cragaidh and Beinn Smeorail to name but two, though they have no vertical aspirations beyond 1,500 feet. Also in view to the west is Clynelish Distillery, originally an enterprise of the 1st Duke of Sutherland, but much modernised in the 1960s. Beyond Dalchalm establishes a relationship with the coast which continues as far as Helmsdale. Gorgeous beaches, devoid of even Man Friday footprints, characterise the next ten miles, with enough flotsam and jetsam deposited on their pristine sands and shingle to provide a decent living for an ambitious beachcomber.

**Sutherland Coastline** - *This page:* between Golspie and Brora with Dunrobin Castle and Ben Bhraggie in the distance. *Opposite:* shingle at Portgower.

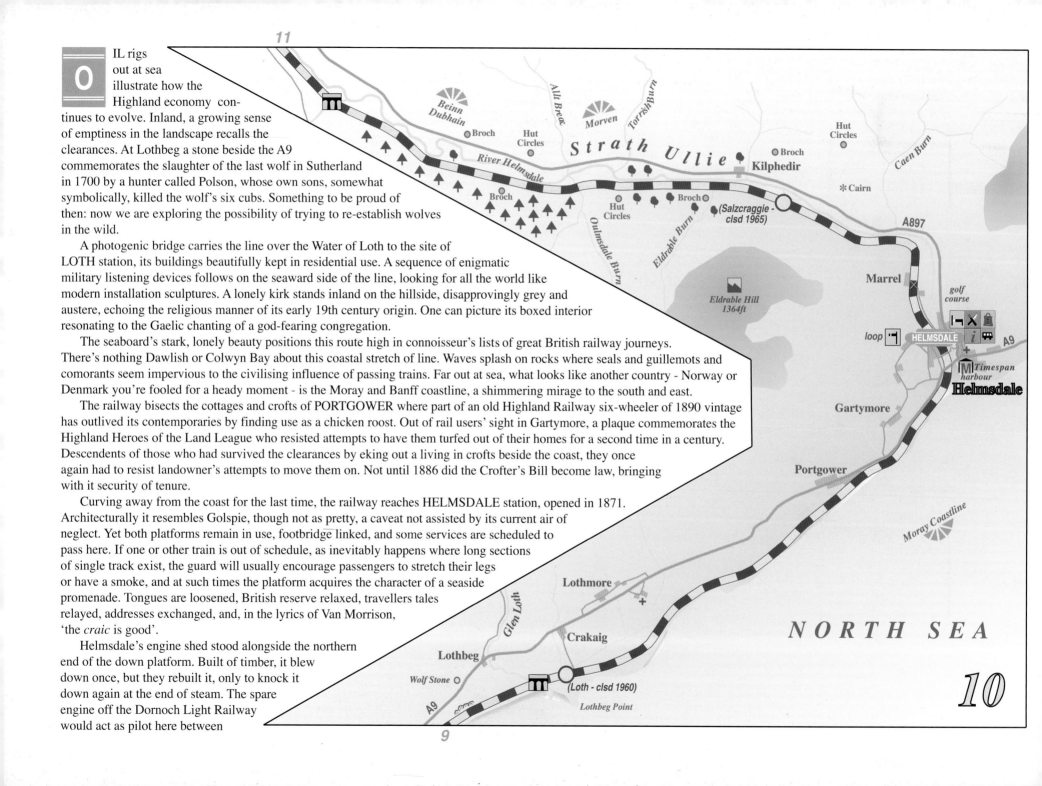

Oil rigs out at sea illustrate how the Highland economy continues to evolve. Inland, a growing sense of emptiness in the landscape recalls the clearances. At Lothbeg a stone beside the A9 commemorates the slaughter of the last wolf in Sutherland in 1700 by a hunter called Polson, whose own sons, somewhat symbolically, killed the wolf's six cubs. Something to be proud of then: now we are exploring the possibility of trying to re-establish wolves in the wild.

A photogenic bridge carries the line over the Water of Loth to the site of LOTH station, its buildings beautifully kept in residential use. A sequence of enigmatic military listening devices follows on the seaward side of the line, looking for all the world like modern installation sculptures. A lonely kirk stands inland on the hillside, disapprovingly grey and austere, echoing the religious manner of its early 19th century origin. One can picture its boxed interior resonating to the Gaelic chanting of a god-fearing congregation.

The seaboard's stark, lonely beauty positions this route high in connoisseur's lists of great British railway journeys. There's nothing Dawlish or Colwyn Bay about this coastal stretch of line. Waves splash on rocks where seals and guillemots and comorants seem impervious to the civilising influence of passing trains. Far out at sea, what looks like another country - Norway or Denmark you're fooled for a heady moment - is the Moray and Banff coastline, a shimmering mirage to the south and east.

The railway bisects the cottages and crofts of PORTGOWER where part of an old Highland Railway six-wheeler of 1890 vintage has outlived its contemporaries by finding use as a chicken roost. Out of rail users' sight in Gartymore, a plaque commemorates the Highland Heroes of the Land League who resisted attempts to have them turfed out of their homes for a second time in a century. Descendents of those who had survived the clearances by eking out a living in crofts beside the coast, they once again had to resist landowner's attempts to move them on. Not until 1886 did the Crofter's Bill become law, bringing with it security of tenure.

Curving away from the coast for the last time, the railway reaches HELMSDALE station, opened in 1871. Architecturally it resembles Golspie, though not as pretty, a caveat not assisted by its current air of neglect. Yet both platforms remain in use, footbridge linked, and some services are scheduled to pass here. If one or other train is out of schedule, as inevitably happens where long sections of single track exist, the guard will usually encourage passengers to stretch their legs or have a smoke, and at such times the platform acquires the character of a seaside promenade. Tongues are loosened, British reserve relaxed, travellers tales relayed, addresses exchanged, and, in the lyrics of Van Morrison, 'the *craic* is good'.

Helmsdale's engine shed stood alongside the northern end of the down platform. Built of timber, it blew down once, but they rebuilt it, only to knock it down again at the end of steam. The spare engine off the Dornoch Light Railway would act as pilot here between stints on the branch. And in common with The Mound, Helmsdale was a spot where restaurant cars were uncoupled from northbound trains, victualled and revitalised before being joined to southbound services.

A fundamental change comes over the landscape as the railway twists inland, forging a path up the valley of the River Helmsdale, or Strath Ullie as it is also known. You haven't travelled far before you see the first of many ruined crofts abandoned after the cruel clearances of the early 19th century. They hug the lineside at Marrel and explain the solitary remoteness of the river valley, which bears more evidence of ancient man than our relatively recent forebears. Cleared for sheep which couldn't flourish on the inhospitable moorlands, the countryside came into its own during the second half of the 19th century as the railway opened it up to the hunting, shooting, fishing fraternity. Request stops opened to serve hunting lodges and shooting boxes built by rich industrialists from the south, and the Highland Railway was happy to profit from their retinues. These lonely platforms have gone, but the salmon beats remain, and you won't go far in season without encountering dry-fly fishermen at their sport, only sadly now they mostly come in 4x4s, luggage racks no longer suspiciously dripping their scaley contents on the unsuspecting heads of fellow passengers. No more the shooting-brakes, drawn up in the station yard at Helmsdale, to collect their wealthy patrons off the morning connection with the sleeper at Inverness.

Social history and politics apart, this really is a lovely stretch of railway line, in total contrast to the seaside stage of the journey preceeding it, but equally enjoyable. Fishing on the river is divided into upper and lower beats with an evocative nomenclature to match: Sand Pool, Nuttings Streams, Tail of the Park, Lone Tree Pool, One Minute Hole, Poachers, Ewes Neuk, The Foam, Craggie Bend, Vale of Tears, Dog's Nose. Does not romance, however subconscious, beat in the heart of every angler? It certainly did in the ample bosom of Barbara Cartland, who once had a house at Kilphedir.

**Strath Ullie** - early morning mist fills the valley

**Strath of Kildonan** - all quiet on the down platform, Kildonan

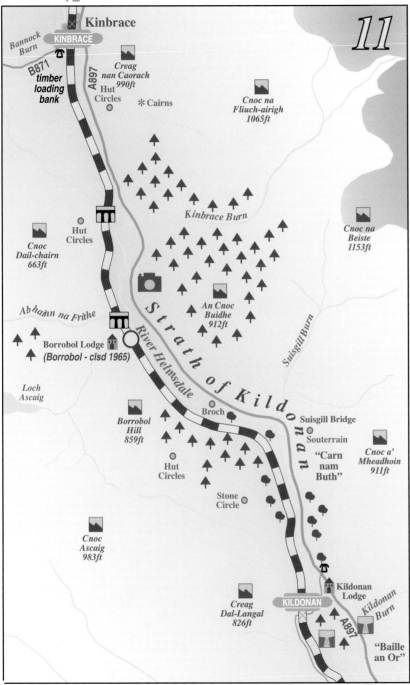

**W**E'RE a tad late for the Kildonan Gold Rush of 1869, just as it was too early to take advantage of the railway. The *Illustrated London News* of 29th May that year reported that the two omnibuses which ran daily up from Helmsdale were always overcrowded and that it was a pity that the railway was, as yet, incomplete. A man who had returned from the Australian gold fields took one look at the Strath of Kildonan and reckoned 'there was gold in them there hills'. In double quick time five hundred born optimists were panning for gold in the Kildonan and Kinbrace burns. They lived, Klondyke style, in huts and tents, but within a year the Duke of Sutherland was ordering the prospectors off his land, his ghillies were concerned about the adverse effect all this hubbub was having on game. The bubble had, not surprisingly, burst. Yet you can still go panning for gold in Kildonan Burn (subject to a strenuous list of conditions issued by the Sutherland Estates) in the vicinity of Baille an Or, the town of gold. Just don't expect to make your fortune!

Overlooking the confluence of Kildonan Burn and the main river, the parish kirk is of 18th century origin, a plaque within commemorates settlers in Canada cleared from Kildonan in 1813. At KILDONAN there is an unusual reversal in precedence and protocol - the train must stop at the level crossing to check that no road vehicle is approaching and not the other way around. A charming Highland Railway timber waiting room adorns the down platform, only there is no loop here now. Masked by trees, Kildonan Lodge dates from the late 19th century. More elaborate than earlier shooting boxes, which were largely confined to gentlemanly pursuits, the bigger lodges such as this were built as their womenfolk began to demand a role in the proceedings. As the river descends, sometimes creaming over falls, the railway climbs. For over a mile between Kildonan and the old halt at Borrobol, the gradient is as steep as 1 in 60. At Suisgill there was another gold rush settlement called Carn nam Buth - the city of tents. Just south of Suisgill Bridge lies a well-preserved souterrain, an Iron Age underground larder, but also a useful place in which to hide from your enemies or the rent collector. The surrounding area is a good place to look through the carriage window for deer. Two hills become prominent landmarks ahead as the train proceeds up the valley.

Borrobol Lodge is another late 19th century shooting box. It stands in an attractive setting sheltered by trees and has a curious little walled garden with a gazebo. You may also catch a glimpse of the old platform, which remained in use until the mid 1960s. Also to be seen are ghillies cottages and kennels, whilst on the eastern side of the line stands one of a number of prefabricated buildings erected out of timber and corrugated-iron which are a feature of the area. In *Sutherland - an Architectural Guide* (Rutland Press 1995) Elizabeth Beaton suggests that these were supplied by Spiers & Co of Glasgow early in the 20th century, who advertised them as being ideal for schools, drill halls, reading rooms and sanatoria, and that they came ready-equipped with automatic dry earth closets. Undoubtedly the components would have reached the Highlands by rail.

Crossing the River Helmsdale, which flows down out of a series of lochs to the north-west, the railway approaches KINBRACE. But before the train reaches the station, an intriguing row of stacked timber might well catch the eye of passengers on the left hand side of the train. This is a pioneering Highland Rail Partnership scheme to transport timber from landlocked forests in the area to factories near Inverness. Uniquely, the timber trains load by night when no other trains are using the line, obviating the need to go to the expense of building a loop or a siding. Five consecutive nights a month, seven or eight months a year, a Canadian built EWS Class 66 locomotive comes up from Inverness in the evening, runs round its train of 21 OTA wagons at Forsinard and returns to the loading bank at Kinbrace. 450 tonnes of timber are then grab-loaded on to the train in an operation lasting around four hours. The train is back in Inverness by 6.30am the following morning, a highly innovative and welcome use of rail transport.

**T**HOSE twin peaks which have been shadowing your climb through the Strath of Kildonan now reveal themselves as the Ben Griam brothers, More and Beg; not even Corbetts of 2,000 feet or more, but the highest peaks in Flow Country. The Scottish Mountaineering Club's District Guidebook briefly notes that these twin cones of Old Red Sandstone are conspicuous landmarks and that Ben Griam Beg is an important archaeological site, having on its summit the remains of the highest hill fort in Scotland.

Flow Country? This is the name given to the vast tract of peatland shared by Sutherland and Caithness that your train is now crossing, essentially a huge sponge! Miles and miles of green mosses and brown grasses, adorned by white bog cotton, extend to an horizon framed by the carriage window. Apart from anglers, and stalkers with high velocity rifles, the occupants of this stark landscape are predominantly equipped with wings: buzzards, geese, dunlin, golden plover, greenshank and, if you are lucky, hen-harriers and even eagles.

Crossing Bannock Burn the railway runs along a large expanse of water called Loch an Ruathair overlooked by Creag Sail a' Bhathaich. Boats dragged up into the grass at the edge of the loch suggest that it's worth fishing, perhaps the rights belong to the occupant of Achentoul Lodge, that whitewashed house to the east of the A897. Snow fences line the track, or at least the eroded remains of them. Some were simply palisades of old sleepers designed so that driven snow would gather against them rather than block the track. Often more than one line of snow fencing was built to provide more than one obstacle for snow storms. But the Highland Railway also adopted a system, developed by a Lancashire man called Howie, of 'blowers' or angled troughs which, when erected alongside the track at the points which experience had shown to be the most prone to drifting, would deflect the wind in such a manner as to prevent the snow packing. Not that the railway authorities could ever hope to completely counteract the effects of snowfall in this inhospitable part of the Highlands, and various designs of snow ploughs for fitting to locomotives were an early priority for the Highland Railway's first locomotive engineer, William Stroudley. Despite such efforts, however, down the years there have been many instances of trains being caught in giant drifts, for hours or even days at a time. In 1895 a fish train was stranded near Forsinard for ten days, but when at last the line was cleared the fish remained in perfect condition, the snow drifts having acted as an effective refrigerator. As recently as 2001 a diesel unit was trapped in snow falls near Kinbrace for six hours. Its eighteen passengers, two ScotRail crew-members and CCG trolley-attendant were rescued in the middle of the night by workers from the Borrobol estate equipped with an ex Army Snowcat.

The lonely station at FORSINARD brings with it the welcome feeling of an oasis in a desert . Civilisation is restricted to just two houses, an hotel and the station building itself, but in the context of what has gone before it might be Sauchiehall Street. The loop remains an important passing point and both platforms are in use. A small timber waiting room suffices for protection against the elements on the up platform. The main station building on the down platform is enjoying a new lease of life as a visitor centre for the Royal Society for the Protection of Birds Forsinard Nature Reserve. The reserve opened in 1995 and has been going from strength to strength ever since. It covers 17,500 acres including the Dubh Lochan Trail, a mile long waymarked pathway which introduces you to many aspects of this peatland landscape. One unnecessarily melancholy feature of Forsinard station is, however, its boarded up signal box, a true Highland Railway survivor and one of a pair which once controlled the station's signalling arrangements. Its twin was demolished when semaphore signalling was replaced by radio control, but in common HR practice there was also signalling equipment in the station building, two levers manufactured by Dutton & Co of Worcester remaining in place in curious juxtaposition to the visitor centre's flora and fauna exhibits. Forsinard retains an engineering siding accessed by a groundframe. In the railway's heyday some unusual consignments were regularly loaded here: peat for transport south to various distilleries; crates of rabbits; and sphagnum mosses for use as wound dressings during the two world wars. Powers to construct a Forsinard, Melvich & Port Skerra Light Railway were obtained in 1898. Materials were delivered but work never commenced. Pity, that!

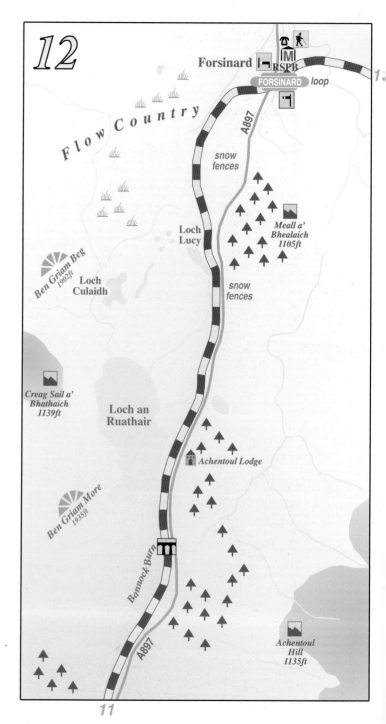

*12*

Forsinard

RSPB

FORSINARD *loop*

*Flow Country*

A897

snow fences

Meall a' Bhealaich
1105ft

Ben Griam Beg
1902ft

Loch Lucy

Loch Culaidh

snow fences

Creag Sail a' Bhathaich
1139ft

Loch an Ruathair

Achentoul Lodge

Ben Griam More
1935ft

Bannock Burn

Achentoul Hill
1135ft

A897

**Flow Country** - the 'Safeway Flyer' passing Loch an Ruathair

**Back of Beyond** - a southbound train slows to pick up a lone walker at Altnabreac

**A**S if there was a bit of an altercation back at Forsinard, road and rail go their own ways, the A897 making more or less due north, the railway veering in an easterly direction, its remoteness redoubled by the separation. Altnabreac notwithstanding, the seventeen miles to Scotscalder redefine all the words the dictionary can muster meaning lonely. None of them seem adequate. Roger Lloyd in his 1953 book *Railwaymen's Gallery* suggested that there was a sense of menace about it. L. T. C. Rolt in *Lines of Character* (published the year before) likened the landscape to a dark and stormy sea. Some hack called Pearson wrote in *Railway Holiday in Scotland* (Wayzgoose 2001) that the emptiness was snow-blinding in its intensity. You may have your own, better, analogies. Suffice it to say that the railway briefly encounters a wilderness of almost Trans-Siberian immensity that you will recall in retrospect with affection equal to anything that has gone before.

And yet, and yet, there is something suspicious about this landscape. Something not quite right. Those Colonel Blimp-like figures, sitting across the aisle, and reactionary enough to still be using the Ordnance Survey one inch map No.11, are disorientated. Where have all these conifer trees come from? They weren't here in 1956! No more they were. They are the indiscriminate harvest of mass plantings in the 1980s as the Government, keen to replenish timber resources exhausted by the demands of two world wars, encouraged private investment in forestry with tax loopholes. A forestry boom ensued, and creative accountants of many wealthy businessmen, show business celebrities and sporting personalities encouraged their clients to invest in burgeoning plantations of non-indigenous, fast-growing species of conifer tree - spruces, sitka and lodgepole pine - which had an adverse effect on the peatlands of the Flow Country, unbalancing the area's natural drainage pattern and unsettling the native flora and fauna. Only recently, as conservationists have eventually been able to convince those in authority of the damage, has this process been reversed, and a strategy devised for returning this landscape to its original condition of blanket bog. It will take time, over thirty years of a myopic planting policy cannot be altered overnight. But many of the trees will be harvested during the next few years and it would be nice to believe that they will all go by rail!

A 1 in 60 climb carries the Far North line up to its second, and highest summit at County March, the old boundary between Sutherland and Caithness. Clearing the summit the train's speed increases palpably, and it rockets down to Altnabreac with the wheels hitting the rail joints in a satisfyingly traditional rhythm, and for a moment you can almost persuade yourself that there's a 'Black Five' up at the front and that there's a Lyons boxed fruit pie waiting to be devoured in your haversack.

ALTNABREAC echoes the West Highland halt at Corrour in its isolation: no metalled roads here, just fudge-coloured tracks wending their way over the bog and through the conifer plantations. So back of beyond is the setting the railway authorities have absent-mindedly allowed the old down side water tower to remain undemolished, a three-dimensional tribute to the generations of steam leviathans which paused here to take a drink, whilst on the up side a water crane lies where it was allowed to fall. Those who have chosen to alight may momentarily feel a sense of panic. The sound of the disappearing train diminishes and you are left in the company of ... a *telling* silence.

*13*

Loch Meadhoin

Loch a Chiteadh

Loch an Duine

Lochan Dubh a Chracairnie

Loch Losgann

Cnoc Beul na Faire 657ft

Caol Loch

Lochan Dubh nan Geodh

Loch Eileanach

Skyline Loch

Garbh Loch

Loch Gaineimh

Loch Caise

Cnoc Maol Donn 606ft

Sleach Water

ALTNABREAC

Clar Loch

Lochdhu Lodge

Loch Dubh

County March Summit - 708ft

snow fences

Cnoc nan Gall 902ft

Loch Eun

Loch a Mhadaidh

Loch Rumsdale

snow fences

Scotscalder - Ben Dorrery beyond

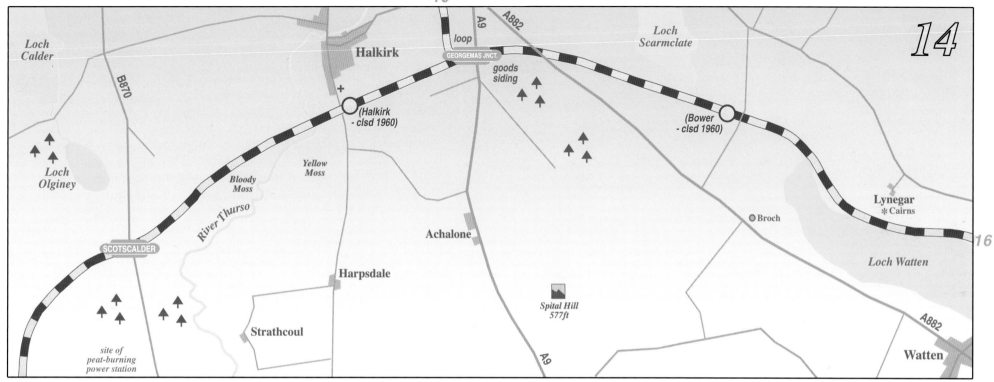

N any other context, SCOTSCALDER would be viewed as isolated, here it returns a reassuring sense of civilisation. Only you do wonder, if someone has requested the train to stop and you see the old-fashioned nature of the station furniture, if you have not, in the foreboding expanses of Flow Country, somehow passed through a time warp and turned the clock back fifty years. But there is a rational explanation! Scotscalder station is now in private hands, having been purchased from British Rail in 1988 for an unspecified sum plus a pound for every mile it stood from Euston, and at certain times this beautifully and nostalgically restored station is available for holiday let under the auspices of the Small Stations Society.

At Braehour, to the south of Scotscalder, a peat-burning power station was optimistically erected in 1956. A network of narrow gauge railways - totalling some four miles in extent - was built to deliver peat to the generating unit, and a Ruston & Hornsby diesel locomotive purchased to provide motive power. Unfortunately the pioneering process was not a success and the project was abandoned around 1961.

Why Scotscalder remained open whilst Halkirk - with at least a decently sized (grid-plan) settlement on its doorstep - closed, is a not untypical railway mystery. Probably it was deemed too near to Britain's most northerly railway junction at GEORGEMAS. Here, until 1995, it

was the practice to split Far North trains into Wick and Thurso portions. Now the old ritual has been by-passed by the simple expedient of reversing the diesel unit down to Thurso first and then running it back through Georgemas Junction to finish its four hour journey from Inverness at Wick. Irrefutable accountancy - it obviates the need for a second crew - but a dilution of railway tradition for those who hitherto had enjoyed watching the trains split, and seeing another locomotive couple up to the Thurso carriages. Back in 1951, Rolt was enraptured to find a Highland 'Ben' waiting to do the honours, and he and his companion, Patrick Whitehouse - later to find fame as one half of the production team on BBC's *Railway Roundabout* - cadged a swaying footplate ride aboard *Ben Alder* for the seven mile run to Britain's most northerly bufferstops. These days Georgemas Junction is a pale and somewhat squalid shadow of its former self, but at least it's enjoying a new lease of life as a freight depot. Six days a week, EWS's 'Safeway Flyer' arrives at the end of its overnight journey up from the outskirts of Glasgow with fresh containers bound for the Safeway supermarkets at Wick and Thurso on the mainland, and Kirkwall on the Orkney Isles. It is heartening to see rail freight being successfully used in this manner, and good that a local firm of refrigerator manufacturers also make use of the service, but if this can happen in somewhere as far flung as Caithness, why not in Penzance, Aberystwyth and Scarborough?

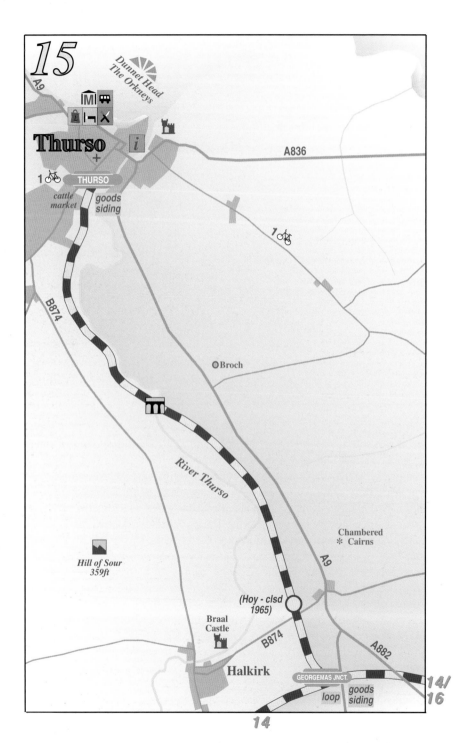

**D**ERELICT air-raid shelters beside the site of the old station at Hoy put you in mind of how significant to the military authorities of two world wars, the Far North line was. Huge long troop trains and naval specials ran through both wars, ferrying soldiers and sailors to and from Scapa Flow, the Royal Navy's natural anchorage in the Orkney Isles. These 'Jellicoes' (which got their name from the First World War Admiral responsible for the Grand Fleet) ran from London Euston through to Thurso, a journey of 717 miles accomplished - if there were no delays - in under 22 hours. 'Jellicoe' was the polite name for them, 'Misery' their more colloquial sobriquet.

Running down through the valley of the River Thurso - which flows out of Loch More not far from Altnabreac - the train beats out a *rallentando* rhythm, a coda-like accompaniment to its journey's end. The Caithness countryside has bottomed out, its rolling hills vertically challenged at four hundred feet. There are cattle in the fields now, fields delineated by flagstone walling. Like the past, Caithness is another country, they do things differently here. A girder bridge carries the line across the river, wide at this point and frequently fished. Thurso's church spires and towers appear on the horizon. Those in the know start reaching down their luggage.

The Sutherland & Caithness Railway reached THURSO in 1874, the Highland Railway had subscribed £50,000 towards its capital cost, the 3rd Duke of Sutherland £10,000 more. It has remained Britain's most northerly terminus ever since, but might have lost that claim had late 19th century proposals for an extension along the coast to Dunnet and Gills Bay, together with a spur to the port of Scrabster materialised. These were revived after the First World War, when a considerable amount of surplus railway material was being returned from the front lines in France, and when the railways' strategic role as a means of transport was still fresh in the memory.

Look out for a cemetery on your right, beyond the river. Because it was on steeply sloping ground, rails were laid on either side of the burial plots and winch-operated wagons employed to remove spoil from freshly dug graves. 154 miles after leaving Inverness, the train enters Thurso station, coming to a halt past a large cattle market on the left hand side and a small goods yard on the right. In terms of volume of trade, the cattle market once kept the railway as busy as the one at Lairg. The goodsyard, on the other hand, only recently revived, struggles to be a viable entity and will need nurturing to survive. As an architectural statement, Thurso station doesn't let you down. You deserve something better than a bus shelter for travelling this far, and you get it. A train-shed establishes a sense of gravitas, and it is reassuring to find a booking-hall (or travel centre in marketing-speak) with a friendly, patient and knowledgeable face behind the counter, especially if you have come all the way from Iceland or Peru, as many seem to do. On the way back, from wherever you've been, spare some time to take in the detail: the sandstone used in the single-storey building's construction, the rounded windows, the long, low, lean-to provided for office accommodation. A run-round loop remains in situ for visiting excursion trains and the few goods which come down from Georgemas Junction. A Highland Railway timber goods shed survives also, though, regrettably, the stone-built engine shed was being slowly demolished in 2003. As you step off the train and walk towards the doors giving access to the street, beyond the buffer-stops you come upon a mural of an old David Jones outside cylinder 4-4-0 called *Caithness*. It was built by Dubs & Co of Glasgow in 1874. It's an elegant wee engine, and you can't help wishing it had hauled you down from Georgemas on horsehair upholstery in a compartment of richly veneered teak. But at least we still have the railway. And long may that remain the case.

**Journey's End -** *Main picture:* crossing the River Thurso.
*Insets:* buffer stops, Thurso station

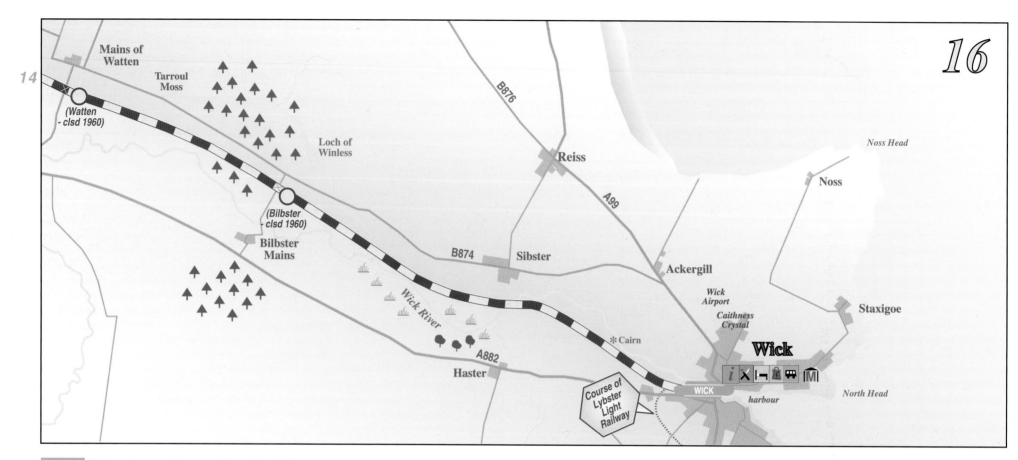

I F there is a sneaking suspicion of anti-climax governing the fourteen miles between Georgemas Junction and Wick you should do your best to put it to the back of your mind. Wick may lack Thurso's kudos of being furthest north, but the journey isn't entirely without interest, and having come this far it would be remiss of you not to explore what was traditionally considered the 'main line' in contrast to Thurso's branch status.

Beyond Loch Watten the railway crosses Tarroul Moss, low-lying, tussocky and emblazoned by gorse in early summer. On the south-western horizon sugar-loaf Morven and pointed Maiden Pap inscrutably watch over the completion of your journey. It is three hours since you first glimpsed Morven on the way out of Tain. At 2,313 feet it is the highest point in Caithness.

The level crossing at BILBSTER is still protected by gates. Wick River, which has flowed out of Loch Watten, accompanies the line through a tract of marshland before passing beneath the railway near Sibster. A monument commemorating one of the last clan battles overlooks the line as the train slows for Wick. This one was between the Campbells and the Sinclairs

on the 13th July, 1680, but there are a number of such monuments in Scotland, and it would be a brave expert who pronounced for once and all the date and site of the clan battle to end all clan battles, particularly as Rangers and Celtic still play each other at least four times a football season.

The Wick & Lybster Light Railway opened in 1903 and closed in 1944, illustrating how difficult it would have been for all the other light railways proposed in the northern highlands to sustain viability. But while it lasted it was a characterful line, as celebrated in Iain Sutherland's self-published book *The Wick & Lybster Railway* which is available locally. 13 miles and 63 chains long, the names of its stations and halts have a poetic intensity about them: Thrumster, Welsh's Crossing, Ulbster, Mid Clyth, Roster Road, Occumster, Parkside Halt, Plantation Level Crossing, Lybster - 'all change, all change'. Drive down the A99 now and you'll have no trouble tracing the route of the line. Several buildings remain - Lybster station is now the club house of the local golf course! For a while the Wick & Lybster successfully carried fish. But in the second half of its life it enjoyed a more unusual role, for Wick had declared itself an officially alcohol free town in May 1921, and each Saturday special trains were laid on to carry a thirsty exodus down to Lybster's famous Bay View Hotel, colloquially known after its entrepreneurial proprietress as 'Maggie Donn's'.

There's a distinct sense of *deja vu* about arriving at WICK. You think you're back at Thurso in a remake of *Groundhog Day*. You want to seek out Andie MacDowell and drink a toast to World Peace. The thing is that Wick and Thurso stations bear a striking resemblance.

The same platform arrangement, the same train-shed, the same mural of No.68 *Caithness* beyond the buffer-stops. And then it dawns on you that Thurso is built out of sandstone, whereas Wick is in Caithness flagstone. You can point that out to your new-found friends from Connecticut ... there are *bound* to be some!

**Loch Watten** - Morven on the horizon.

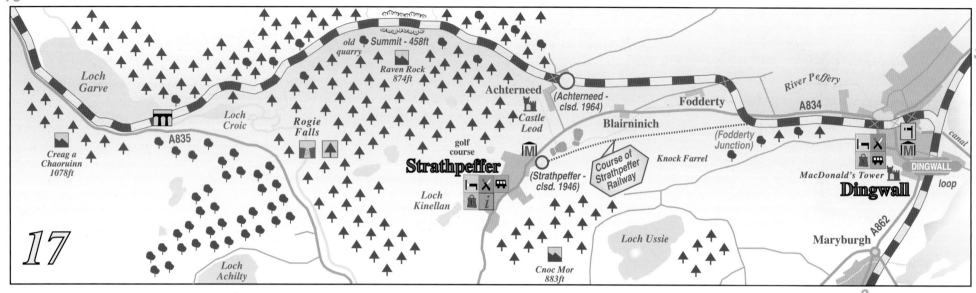

17

**T** HE ritual of point setting repeated - see Map 2 - Kyle bound trains cross the Dingwall Canal before veering left across marshland on what amounts to the first of the route's many tortuous curves. Squealing wheel flanges are replaced by level-crossing sirens as the train gingerly negotiates a trio of roads, passes a municipal park, a disused signal cabin, and a small industrial estate before Dingwall is left behind and the line moves out into the broadening valley of the River Peffery.

All seems set fair for the west until the line suddenly turns sharply to the north, crossing the valley on a sizeable embankment. Railway engineers didn't go in for sharp curves of twenty chains and earthworks if they could avoid them. The obstacle in their path wasn't geological, it was the local laird, Sir William MacKenzie, who insisted that if the railway was to cross the policies of his house at Coul, it would have to be heavily landscaped and passed through an otherwise unnecessary 500 yard long tunnel at its closest point to Coul House. MacKenzie's obstinacy wasn't without irony, as he had put his name to the railway's provisional prospectus.

Briefly, consideration was given to re-routing the line from Conon Bridge (Map 2) to Garve by a more southerly course, but in the event Sir William's intransigence was circumnavigated by taking the line across the valley at Fodderty and passing to the north of his land. Money and face were thus saved, but only at the expense of a daunting gradient of 1 in 50 to Raven Rock, which was to be the scene, on 25th September 1897, of an alarming runaway incident. A coupling snapped on a mixed train, struggling on wet rails to reach the summit, and several wagons and carriages ran loose, gaining speed on the incline, but luckily managing to stay on the track despite the reverse curves between Achterneed and Fodderty. The Highland Railway had a reputation for luck where tragedy was concerned, and, true to form, they escaped on this occasion, the runaway, merely smashing through the level crossing

gates on the outskirts of Dingwall and coming to a halt two hundred yards from the junction with the Far North line, where, in less fortunate circumstances, collision with another train could well have occurred.

Ironically, Sir William MacKenzie didn't live to see the opening of the railway to Kyle. Moreover, his heir regarded railways far more favourably, and in due course a branch line was built between Fodderty and Strathpeffer. In an all too brief Edwardian flowering, the branch flourished as holidaymakers flocked to enjoy the delights of this charming little spa. At the zenith of its popularity you could board a sleeping car at Euston and arrive refreshed without change at Strathpeffer's elegant timber station the next morning. A *Strathpeffer Spa Express* operated on Tuesdays, non-stop from Aviemore to Dingwall, and thence to Strathpeffer. Usually, the Highland Railway provided one of David Jones's exceedingly handsome 'Loch' class 4-4-0s to haul this prestigious train, which carried a headboard beneath its unusual louvred chimney, likened by the late, but much venerated, railway historian and artist, Hamilton Ellis, to a ship's funnel. His book, *The Beauty of Old Trains*, is adorned by an atmospheric colour plate of Loch Garve hauling a passenger train near Achnashellach circa 1925. Sadly, only one of Jones's - and, indeed, the Highland's - locomotives survived into preservation, and it wasn't a 'Loch', it was one of his 4-6-0 'Big Goods' engines, now residing in Glasgow's Museum of Transport.

Opened in 1885, the two and a half mile long Strathpeffer branch was closed to passenger trains in 1946, and following the cessation of freight five years later, was subsequently torn up with an urgency often absent from its later years of operation. Half a century later, investigations were being undertaken to see if a reconstructed Strathpeffer branch might once again bring tourism to the re-emergent spa. A report compiled in 2000 by Highland Rail Developments suggested that there were few engineering impediments to relaying the

**Strathpeffer Station** - waiting for the trains to return?

line. Fortunately the original station building at Strathpeffer had survived the demolition one might have expected was its fate. In recent years it has been developed as a successful visitor centre, cafe and craft outlet. Moreover, the Highland Tourist Board offices occupy the former goods yard, so there is every reason to believe that a steam-worked Strathpeffer Railway would attract much interest. At the Fodderty end there are options to provide a simple run-round loop and exchange platform with ScotRail services, or a more ambitious through link to Dingwall and beyond. Integrated transport, or so it seems, is a concept in need of reinvention every fifty years or so!

Before the Strathpeffer branch was built, and for eighteen years after it closed, the lonely hillside station of ACHTERNEED provided the spa with all the rail facilities those in authority considered it deserved. Indeed, Achterneed station was originally named Strathpeffer, albeit a good mile's walk away on the opposite side of the valley. As the train approaches the site of Achterneed station you get a good view across the valley, and can easily trace the trackbed of the Strathpeffer branch making its way beneath the bluebell-carpeted, vitrified fort-topped flank of Knock Farrel. Notice how far the railway has climbed above the river in such a short distance, back at Dingwall you were virtually at sea level, now you are approximately two hundred and fifty feet above it!

There are bluebells also in the cuttings which carry you up to Raven Rock, and, in season, primroses too and broom aplenty. Modern 'Sprinter' trains make comparatively light work of the climb, though you will still be aware of their underfloor engines working to capacity. Diesel locomotive-hauled trains, such as the *Royal Scotsman*, face a noticeably harder task; imagine, then, that the firemen of steam engines had their work cut out to get their fire-box hungry steeds up and over the summit. Often, heavier trains were banked by Dingwall's pilot engine. How sad that the Kyle line doesn't regularly feature steam-hauled excursions so that such scenes can be re-enacted for our entertainment.

The summit at RAVEN ROCK is 458 feet above sea level, and we have climbed to that lofty height in just over six miles. Even higher is the rock itself, menacingly looming over the line, an intimidating presence diluted somewhat in recent times by the growth of vegetation. Legend has it that generations of ravens nested on this precipice, jutting two hundred and fifty feet above the track, until the railway was built, never to return again. Perhaps the railway navvies' gelignite, blasting through intractible shards of gneiss and slate, has remained ever since in tribal memory.

In the 1920s a rail-served quarry was opened on the west side of Raven Rock. Five sidings were laid to cope with the outward traffic, empty wagons being propelled up from the loop at Achterneed. At its peak the quarry employed twenty men and, on average, a train of ten loaded wagons was despatched daily, largely for use in road building. The quarrymen reached their place of work by cycling up a path which ran beside the line from Achterneed. Habitually they would hang on to westbound trains, until a fatality brought such dangerous practices to an abrupt end. Going home they vied with each other to speed down the bank, six minutes reputedly being the record time for the five miles down to Fodderty! The quarry was abandoned at the outset of the Second World War, but you can still see one of the old crushing hoppers, a shadowy remnant in amongst the trees.

You sense the train's relief in breasting the summit. It bowls downhill through dense woodland; initially at 1 in 85, steepening to 1 in 50 - eastbound trains have it no easier. Emerging from the trees the line skirts Loch Garve which feeds a salmon-rich tributary of the River Conon known as the Black Water. In the Gaelic, Garve means 'rough loch', and on tempestuous days the wind can funnel down off the mountains creating a wave-tossed sheet of water. About a mile and a half in length, Loch Garve is over a hundred feet at its deepest point and apparently never totally freezes over. There is probably a good scientific explanation for this, given the extreme nature of Highland winters, but the story goes that the depths of Garve are home to a water kelpie who took a human woman for a wife, and that she insisted on central heating!

**Garve** - what's at the rainbow's end?

**Achanalt** - crossing the bridge between Loch a Chuilinn and Loch Achanalt with Sgurr a' Ghlas Leathaid in the distance

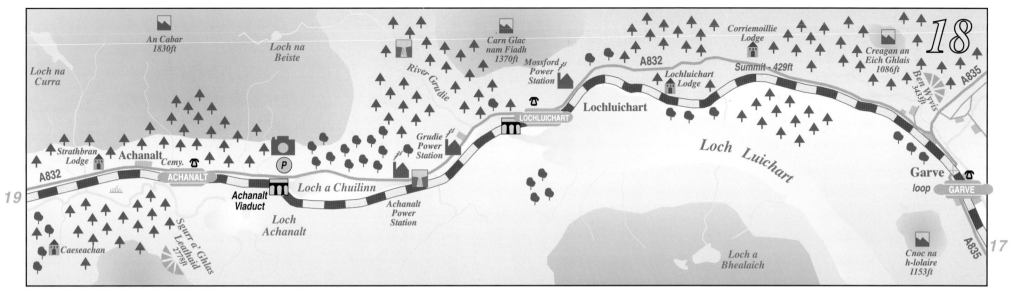

**F**IELDS grazed by sheep and cattle, together with a farm which has seemingly purloined Garve's old signal cabin for indeterminate usage, hasten the railway back to a brief measure of civilisation. Not that GARVE (or Gairbh) offers much by way of incentive to detrain. Even the hotel discourages those who do not arrive by coach and the village shop has bolted its doors for the last time. Perhaps if Garve had become the railway junction once planned it might have grown as a settlement. Twice in the late 19th century a line was proposed which would run in a north-westerly direction from Garve to Ullapool, and in fact the 33 mile route in question got as far as receiving Royal Assent in 1890. Scenically, it would have been a fabulous line. But, of course, its promoters weren't so much interested in scenery as in herrings, though the potential influx of visitors would have also well-suited the good burghers of Ullapool. Fascinatingly, in retrospect, the scheme didn't get built not so much through indifference, or lack of finance, but rather because its realisation became embroiled in a bitter sequence of squabbling brinkmanship between those old rival railway companies, the Highland and the Great North of Scotland. John Thomas, doyen of Scottish railway historians, went into some detail in his peerless (and still in print) book, *The Skye Railway*. Another well documented feature of the railway at Garve is the width between the up and down lines of the loop. Apparently at an early stage in the construction of the route it was envisaged that fishing boats might be conveyed by open wagon from coast to coast to avoid the lengthy and sometimes perilous sea voyage via Cape Wrath and the Pentland Firth. A pair of 15 ton boat cranes were ordered from Cowans Sheldon to lift vessels out of the water and onto the trains at Strome Ferry and Dingwall. But by the time the railway opened in August, 1870, the annual migration of fishing fleets had passed and a memo was passed to the crane-makers requesting that delivery be postponed. Nothing was ever heard of the project again.

Look back over your shoulder as you leave Garve, and you'll catch a glimpse (cloud cover permitting) of Ben Wyvis, a challenging Munro 3,433ft high, and once the subject of an imaginative rack & pinion railway proposal. The train is doing its best to imitate a rack & pinion operation, climbing yet again at 1 in 50 towards its second summit at Corriemoillie. You know you're nearing it when the dormer windows of Corriemoillie Lodge come into view on the right hand side, first of the 'shooting boxes' which define the Kyle line.

Then it's back downhill again, down to the shores of Loch Luichart, scene of an hydro-electric project in 1954 which required the line to be relaid at a higher level as the waters of the loch were raised some twenty-five feet. A section of the old trackbed is still to be seen amongst the lochside trees to the right of the train, but the old station building lies beneath the water now, and its replacement is as ugly as sin. The hydro-electric power stations at Mossford and Grudie derive their energy from lochs in the mountains beyond, huge pipes - which you could drive a Landrover through - abseiling down the hillsides behind the turbine houses. Achanalt Power Station is a more modest affair, and beside it a salmon ladder allows returning fish to reach their spawning ground in Loch a Chuilinn.

Wild moorland becomes the over-riding theme as the railway describes a reverse curve to cross between two lochs and head for the next station of ACHANALT. There was a loop here until 1966 with up and down platforms and a timber station building. Now an incongruously modern shelter - more aesthetically suited, one feels, to the Central Belt than the Highlands -provides the only accommodation for intending passengers, not that there can be many of them, save for students of early aviation history on pilgrimages to visit the grave of the pioneer military airman Bertram Dickinson. Soldier, aviator, explorer, Captain Dickson is credited with drawing the attention of the British Army to the potential of the aeroplane in a military context. In 1910 he flew a Bristol Boxkite over Salisbury Plain to an appreciative audience including Lord Kitchener and Winston Churchill. That Harrier jet which just roared down the strath is his legacy.

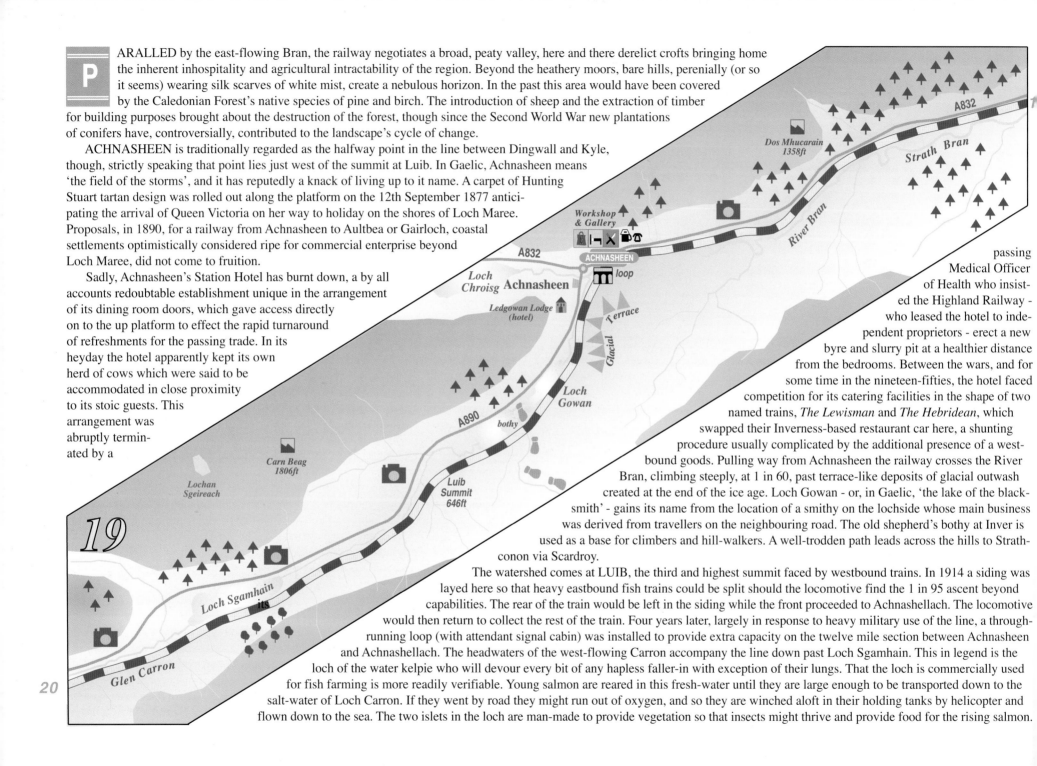

**P** ARALLED by the east-flowing Bran, the railway negotiates a broad, peaty valley, here and there derelict crofts bringing home the inherent inhospitality and agricultural intractability of the region. Beyond the heathery moors, bare hills, perenially (or so it seems) wearing silk scarves of white mist, create a nebulous horizon. In the past this area would have been covered by the Caledonian Forest's native species of pine and birch. The introduction of sheep and the extraction of timber for building purposes brought about the destruction of the forest, though since the Second World War new plantations of conifers have, controversially, contributed to the landscape's cycle of change.

ACHNASHEEN is traditionally regarded as the halfway point in the line between Dingwall and Kyle, though, strictly speaking that point lies just west of the summit at Luib. In Gaelic, Achnasheen means 'the field of the storms', and it has reputedly a knack of living up to it name. A carpet of Hunting Stuart tartan design was rolled out along the platform on the 12th September 1877 anticipating the arrival of Queen Victoria on her way to holiday on the shores of Loch Maree. Proposals, in 1890, for a railway from Achnasheen to Aultbea or Gairloch, coastal settlements optimistically considered ripe for commercial enterprise beyond Loch Maree, did not come to fruition.

Sadly, Achnasheen's Station Hotel has burnt down, a by all accounts redoubtable establishment unique in the arrangement of its dining room doors, which gave access directly on to the up platform to effect the rapid turnaround of refreshments for the passing trade. In its heyday the hotel apparently kept its own herd of cows which were said to be accommodated in close proximity to its stoic guests. This arrangement was abruptly terminated by a

passing Medical Officer of Health who insisted the Highland Railway - who leased the hotel to independent proprietors - erect a new byre and slurry pit at a healthier distance from the bedrooms. Between the wars, and for some time in the nineteen-fifties, the hotel faced competition for its catering facilities in the shape of two named trains, *The Lewisman* and *The Hebridean*, which swapped their Inverness-based restaurant car here, a shunting procedure usually complicated by the additional presence of a westbound goods. Pulling way from Achnasheen the railway crosses the River Bran, climbing steeply, at 1 in 60, past terrace-like deposits of glacial outwash created at the end of the ice age. Loch Gowan - or, in Gaelic, 'the lake of the blacksmith' - gains its name from the location of a smithy on the lochside whose main business was derived from travellers on the neighbouring road. The old shepherd's bothy at Inver is used as a base for climbers and hill-walkers. A well-trodden path leads across the hills to Strathconon via Scardroy.

The watershed comes at LUIB, the third and highest summit faced by westbound trains. In 1914 a siding was layed here so that heavy eastbound fish trains could be split should the locomotive find the 1 in 95 ascent beyond capabilities. The rear of the train would be left in the siding while the front proceeded to Achnashellach. The locomotive would then return to collect the rest of the train. Four years later, largely in response to heavy military use of the line, a through-running loop (with attendant signal cabin) was installed to provide extra capacity on the twelve mile section between Achnasheen and Achnashellach. The headwaters of the west-flowing Carron accompany the line down past Loch Sgamhain. This in legend is the loch of the water kelpie who will devour every bit of any hapless faller-in with exception of their lungs. That the loch is commercially used for fish farming is more readily verifiable. Young salmon are reared in this fresh-water until they are large enough to be transported down to the salt-water of Loch Carron. If they went by road they might run out of oxygen, and so they are winched aloft in their holding tanks by helicopter and flown down to the sea. The two islets in the loch are man-made to provide vegetation so that insects might thrive and provide food for the rising salmon.

**Glen Carron** - looking up the flank of Crag nan Calman

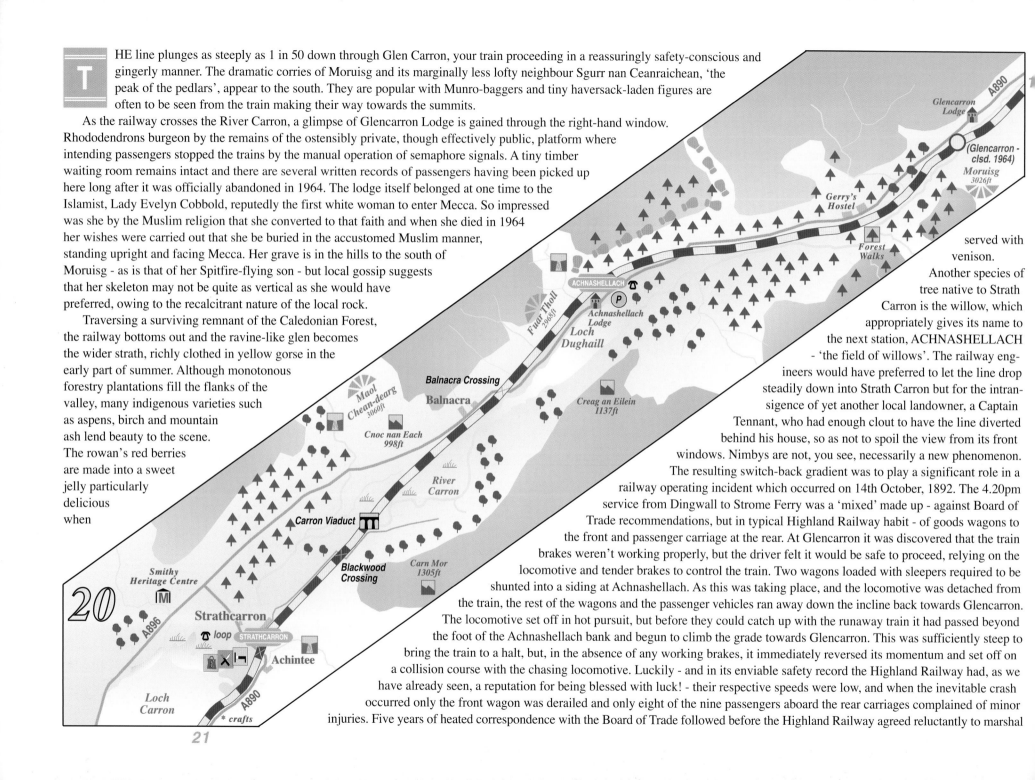

T HE line plunges as steeply as 1 in 50 down through Glen Carron, your train proceeding in a reassuringly safety-conscious and gingerly manner. The dramatic corries of Moruisg and its marginally less lofty neighbour Sgurr nan Ceanraichean, 'the peak of the pedlars', appear to the south. They are popular with Munro-baggers and tiny haversack-laden figures are often to be seen from the train making their way towards the summits.

As the railway crosses the River Carron, a glimpse of Glencarron Lodge is gained through the right-hand window. Rhododendrons burgeon by the remains of the ostensibly private, though effectively public, platform where intending passengers stopped the trains by the manual operation of semaphore signals. A tiny timber waiting room remains intact and there are several written records of passengers having been picked up here long after it was officially abandoned in 1964. The lodge itself belonged at one time to the Islamist, Lady Evelyn Cobbold, reputedly the first white woman to enter Mecca. So impressed was she by the Muslim religion that she converted to that faith and when she died in 1964 her wishes were carried out that she be buried in the accustomed Muslim manner, standing upright and facing Mecca. Her grave is in the hills to the south of Moruisg - as is that of her Spitfire-flying son - but local gossip suggests that her skeleton may not be quite as vertical as she would have preferred, owing to the recalcitrant nature of the local rock.

Traversing a surviving remnant of the Caledonian Forest, the railway bottoms out and the ravine-like glen becomes the wider strath, richly clothed in yellow gorse in the early part of summer. Although monotonous forestry plantations fill the flanks of the valley, many indigenous varieties such as aspens, birch and mountain ash lend beauty to the scene. The rowan's red berries are made into a sweet jelly particularly delicious when

served with venison.

Another species of tree native to Strath Carron is the willow, which appropriately gives its name to the next station, ACHNASHELLACH - 'the field of willows'. The railway engineers would have preferred to let the line drop steadily down into Strath Carron but for the intransigence of yet another local landowner, a Captain Tennant, who had enough clout to have the line diverted behind his house, so as not to spoil the view from its front windows. Nimbys are not, you see, necessarily a new phenomenon. The resulting switch-back gradient was to play a significant role in a railway operating incident which occurred on 14th October, 1892. The 4.20pm service from Dingwall to Strome Ferry was a 'mixed' made up - against Board of Trade recommendations, but in typical Highland Railway habit - of goods wagons to the front and passenger carriage at the rear. At Glencarron it was discovered that the train brakes weren't working properly, but the driver felt it would be safe to proceed, relying on the locomotive and tender brakes to control the train. Two wagons loaded with sleepers required to be shunted into a siding at Achnashellach. As this was taking place, and the locomotive was detached from the train, the rest of the wagons and the passenger vehicles ran away down the incline back towards Glencarron. The locomotive set off in hot pursuit, but before they could catch up with the runaway train it had passed beyond the foot of the Achnashellach bank and begun to climb the grade towards Glencarron. This was sufficiently steep to bring the train to a halt, but, in the absence of any working brakes, it immediately reversed its momentum and set off on a collision course with the chasing locomotive. Luckily - and in its enviable safety record the Highland Railway had, as we have already seen, a reputation for being blessed with luck! - their respective speeds were low, and when the inevitable crash occurred only the front wagon was derailed and only eight of the nine passengers aboard the rear carriages complained of minor injuries. Five years of heated correspondence with the Board of Trade followed before the Highland Railway agreed reluctantly to marshal

20

their mixed trains in accordance with nationally adhered to guidelines.

The Prince of Wales, later King Edward VII, was a guest of Captain Tennant's at Achnashellach Lodge in 1870, soon after the railway had opened. In his honour five hundred deer were driven towards him but he failed to hit one with a single shot. This notorious philanderer's success rate with the female occupants of the area was unfortunately, or perhaps diplomatically, veiled over.

As the train leaves Achnashellach there are dramatic views northwards up the flank of Fuar Tholl - 'the cold hollow' - towards Sgurr Ruadh - 'the red peak'. Many climbers elect to approach these mountains from Achnashellach station. Another popular route is through the Coulin Pass to Glen Torridon, an old pony track followed, in 1803, by Thomas Hogg, the Ettrick Shepherd, during a tour of the Highlands. Beyond Strathcarron, the next station down the line, you can look back on Fuar Tholl and see how it gained its nickname: 'The Duke of Wellington's Nose'.

Still see-sawing with the gradients, but generally descending to the valley floor, the line makes its way through Strath Carron. At Balnacra the A890 swaps sides with the railway by way of a level crossing. Automated now, though when Alexander Frater passed this way in the early Eighties, gleaning copy for a series of Observer colour supplement features which became the delightful book *Stopping Train Britain*, the crossing was still manually operated by a man ever so slightly over-qualified for the position, a Bachelor of Science! Unfortunately his strongly held belief, back then, that it would be more cost effective to employ him for life rather than invest in automation appears to have been misplaced.

Passing drumlins carelessly left behind by the retreating glaciers - ice age litter, you might say - the railway crosses the River Carron and the train slows for Strathcarron. Blackwood level crossing has recently been upgraded with half-barriers for extra protection, somehow British road-users just seem to lack common sense when it comes to crossing railway lines. STRATHCARRON station is the last crossing-place on the route. It also marks the end of the line's inland journeying, for, beyond the level-crossing, the salt-water shores of Loch Carron are reached, and, quite literally, a sea-change comes over the character of the Kyle line!

Balnacra - Loch Dughaill and Creag an Eilein in the background

Inside the inset image:

Achnashellach

**Stop
Look
Listen**

Notify nearest Station Manager
before crossing with a vehicle
which is unusually long, wide,
heavy or slow moving.
Notify Railtrack on
Tel 014 335 2771

1  Open far gate before
   crossing with vehicles
   or animals.

2  Cross quickly.

3  Close and secure gates
   after use.

**Achnashellach -** *Main picture:* crossing the A890
*Inset:* station approach, Fuar Tholl in the clouds

**Badicaul** - looking over the Inner Sound to Raasay and Dun Caan

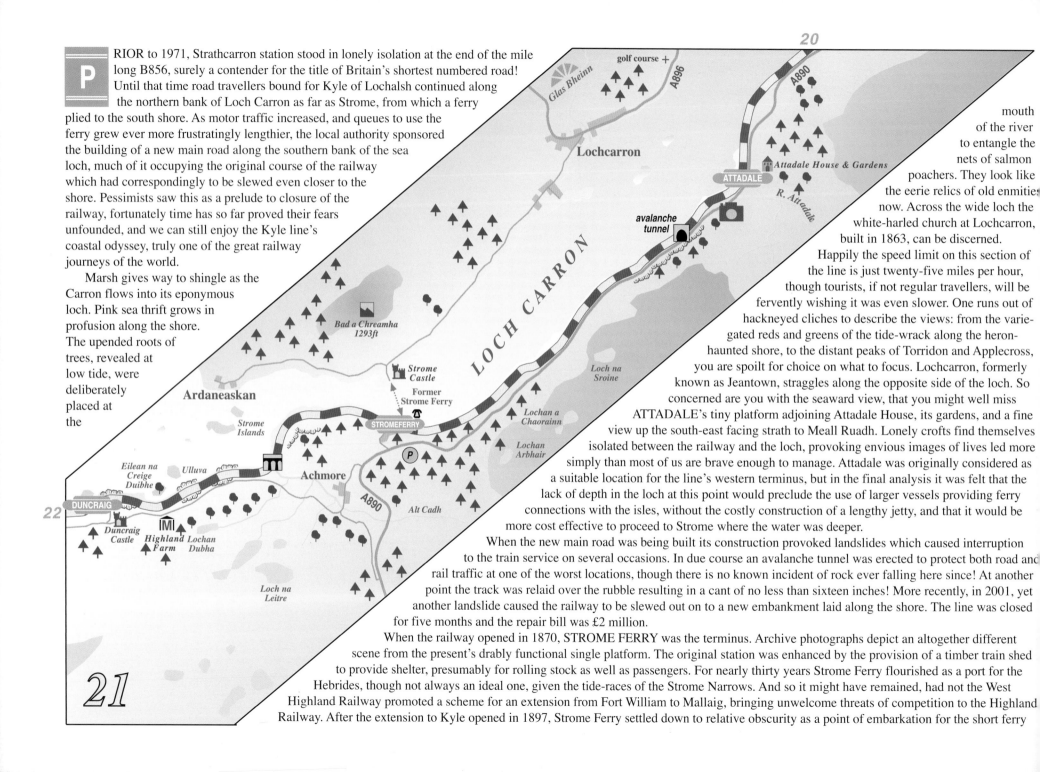

**P**RIOR to 1971, Strathcarron station stood in lonely isolation at the end of the mile long B856, surely a contender for the title of Britain's shortest numbered road! Until that time road travellers bound for Kyle of Lochalsh continued along the northern bank of Loch Carron as far as Strome, from which a ferry plied to the south shore. As motor traffic increased, and queues to use the ferry grew ever more frustratingly lengthier, the local authority sponsored the building of a new main road along the southern bank of the sea loch, much of it occupying the original course of the railway which had correspondingly to be slewed even closer to the shore. Pessimists saw this as a prelude to closure of the railway, fortunately time has so far proved their fears unfounded, and we can still enjoy the Kyle line's coastal odyssey, truly one of the great railway journeys of the world.

Marsh gives way to shingle as the Carron flows into its eponymous loch. Pink sea thrift grows in profusion along the shore. The upended roots of trees, revealed at low tide, were deliberately placed at the mouth of the river to entangle the nets of salmon poachers. They look like the eerie relics of old enmities now. Across the wide loch the white-harled church at Lochcarron, built in 1863, can be discerned.

Happily the speed limit on this section of the line is just twenty-five miles per hour, though tourists, if not regular travellers, will be fervently wishing it was even slower. One runs out of hackneyed cliches to describe the views: from the variegated reds and greens of the tide-wrack along the heron-haunted shore, to the distant peaks of Torridon and Applecross, you are spoilt for choice on what to focus. Lochcarron, formerly known as Jeantown, straggles along the opposite side of the loch. So concerned are you with the seaward view, that you might well miss ATTADALE's tiny platform adjoining Attadale House, its gardens, and a fine view up the south-east facing strath to Meall Ruadh. Lonely crofts find themselves isolated between the railway and the loch, provoking envious images of lives led more simply than most of us are brave enough to manage. Attadale was originally considered as a suitable location for the line's western terminus, but in the final analysis it was felt that the lack of depth in the loch at this point would preclude the use of larger vessels providing ferry connections with the isles, without the costly construction of a lengthy jetty, and that it would be more cost effective to proceed to Strome where the water was deeper.

When the new main road was being built its construction provoked landslides which caused interruption to the train service on several occasions. In due course an avalanche tunnel was erected to protect both road and rail traffic at one of the worst locations, though there is no known incident of rock ever falling here since! At another point the track was relaid over the rubble resulting in a cant of no less than sixteen inches! More recently, in 2001, yet another landslide caused the railway to be slewed out on to a new embankment laid along the shore. The line was closed for five months and the repair bill was £2 million.

When the railway opened in 1870, STROME FERRY was the terminus. Archive photographs depict an altogether different scene from the present's drably functional single platform. The original station was enhanced by the provision of a timber train shed to provide shelter, presumably for rolling stock as well as passengers. For nearly thirty years Strome Ferry flourished as a port for the Hebrides, though not always an ideal one, given the tide-races of the Strome Narrows. And so it might have remained, had not the West Highland Railway promoted a scheme for an extension from Fort William to Mallaig, bringing unwelcome threats of competition to the Highland Railway. After the extension to Kyle opened in 1897, Strome Ferry settled down to relative obscurity as a point of embarkation for the short ferry journey across Loch Carron to North Strome. In the 1970s, however, it became animated once more when new sidings were laid alongside the old jetty for the transfer of cement brought in by rail and loaded onto vessels, which carried it round to an oil rig construction yard on Loch Kishorn. Though relatively short-lived, this unexpected traffic was further instrumental in preventing the line's closure. But perhaps the most curious story concerning Strome Ferry relates to a riot here in 1883, the upshot of protests from devout Presbyterians concerning the working of fish trains on the Sabbath. Over a hundred and fifty angry protesters physically prevented railway workers from transhipping freshly caught fish from the steamers *Harold* and *Lochiel* into waiting railway wagons on the pier. Eight police officers were despatched by special train from Dingwall to quell the disturbance but had little impact in the face of such a large and ugly crowd. Sunday being over, the protesters dutifully retired from the scene on the stroke of midnight. Ten ringleaders were subsequently arrested and tried, and although found guilty were granted clemency on account of their clear religious beliefs. Incidentally, a hundred years were to pass before passenger trains operated on the line on Sundays.

Extending the line from Strome Ferry to Kyle of Lochalsh was no easy matter. The trackbed had to be blasted out of stubborn Torridonian sandstone for most of the way, though at least the spoil from cuttings could be used to build embankments across bays and inlets which characterised the coast. Primitive blasting techniques resulted in a ignificant number of injuries and deaths amongst the workforce, many of whom were local crofters, apt to down tools when farming commitments called. Other navvies hailed from Skye and Ireland,and there was often no love lost

between the differing groups. At least one ill-fated member of the workforce was French, and the site of his death was marked by the naming of a watercourse passing beneath the line as Frenchman's Burn.

An archipelago of tiny islands adds to the interest of the view. On Ulluva a stone cairn was built as a navigational aid. Clothed in Scots pine, Eilean na Creige Duibhe is said to have inspired J. M. Barrie as a setting for the island of the Lost Boys in *Peter Pan* - apparently he often used this line on his way to the Hebrides. Hereabouts, on the mainland shore, don't be shocked to see llamas paddling amongst the rockpools, they will have wandered down from the Highland Farm rare breeds centre. Further out into Loch Carron is the lighthouse on Eilean a Chat, once occupied residentially by the prominent Glaswegian cleric and poet, Lachlan Maclean Watt.

Hugging the shoreline, slipping in and out of vertical cuttings blasted out of sheer rock, and apt to take would-be on-board photographers by surprise - the train, with flanges screeching on the tight curves, continues to the picturesque halt at DUNCRAIG, built for Sir Alexander Matheson, the opium magnate and promoter of the Dingwall & Skye Railway, whose fortress-like castle perches above the headland. Spookily empty now, it served as a naval hospital during the Second World War, and subsequently became a college devoted to domestic science, which meant that the little station became frequented by large parties of giggling maidens, viewed as something of a bonanza by the young bloods of Plockton, who were all reputed to be expert rowers.

**Attadale -** The Royal Scotsman skirts Loch Carron with Fuar Tholl in the distance

**S**PELLBINDINGLY, the train continues past Plockton Bay, its picturesque views brought to a wider audience by BBC's television series *Hamish Macbeth*. Boat trips to see the seals and otters have helped turn Plockton from a village concerned with fishing and crofting into a genteel tourist resort, though fishing for prawns happily remains a viable activity on Loch Carron.

So PLOCKTON is likely to be one of the busiest stops between Dingwall and Kyle. Certainly its station is lent vivacity by the presence of an excellent restaurant in the Highland Railway style timber station building, and bustle by the proximity of a popular bunkhouse effectively erected in a pastiche of a signal box.

Switch-backing gradients lead to DUIRINISH, the penultimate station on the line. Here, during the Second World War, extra sidings were laid for the storage of wagons carrying mines. A more traditional aspect of life in Duirinish is the crofting strips, still visibly worked between the railway and the sea. Railway employees' cottages remain intact adjacent to the now bare platform. Traditionally railwaymen would supplement their income by crofting. Not many people get off at Duirinish. You might buck the trend and make your way down to the shore where otters are not unknown.

Curving south away from Duirinish, the line offers more intoxicating vistas out to sea: in the near distance lie the Crowlin Islands, famed for their seal population; in the middle distance the Isle of Raasay, immediately recognisable by the raked, ship funnel-like protrusion of its highest summit, Dun Caan; and beyond, Skye itself and the fabled Cuillins, and it's a hard-hearted visitor - or staunch Hanoverian - who doesn't find themselves humming softly the gentle refrain of the *Skye Boat Song*.

By the time it reaches Erbusaig Bay, the train is surprisingly heading in a south-easterly direction and you might be astonished to discover that you are now on a more southerly latitude than Inverness. Portnacloich cutting is the deepest and longest on the line. The train emerges from the cutting to slice across Erbusaig Bay on an embankment built from its spoil. Through the carriage window the cluster of houses looks positively

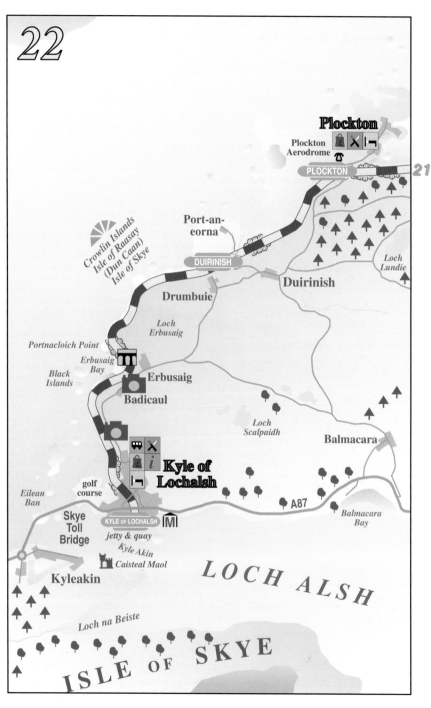

idyllic, but the crofters had their fishing disrupted by the advent of the railway, not to mention their view. As the railway was being constructed, the remains of Viking longboats were unearthed at Erbusaig.

Barely a few minutes of the journey remain, but like the injury time of a close-fought football match, this is no time to leave your seats. Rounding yet another curve, Skye's controversial Toll Bridge is revealed. The bridge has its detractors and supporters; the latter mostly local were it not for the high tolls, necessary if the bridge is ever to defray its construction costs, let alone the interest on those monies. Romantics, with no care for the logistic improvements the structure has brought to the locality, prefer that islands are obligatorily approached afloat. The arguments rumble on, against hopes that the Scottish Parliament might step in and underwrite the tolls.

One doubts, crofting apart, if the railway's coming to Kyle was ever perceived so contentiously. It represented progress with a capital P. Oozing confidence its builders blasted their way through impenetrable layers of gneiss and quartz and erected an elegant pavilion-like timber station jutting boldly out into Kyle Akin. Not considering the hamlet of Kyle grandiose enough for the name of their terminus, they invented the name of KYLE OF LOCHALSH, and so officially it remains, albeit colloquially truncated to just plain 'Kyle'.

It only remains for you to get down on to the platform and soak up the atmosphere before - given this region's reputation for rain - it soaks you. Hopefully, you might encounter some maritime activity - the Navy test torpedoes here! If time is of the essence, then at least spend a proportion of it in the Station Visitor Centre run by the enthusiastic Friends of the Kyle Line. They share, with you, an overriding interest in the Kyle line's survival and development. In their premises, you will be, quite literally, among friends.

**Badicaul and the Black Islands -** *Main picture:* the first up train of the day makes its way out of Kyle. *Inset:* sea-pinks flowering by an overbridge

# gazetteer

If there is a moral to the Iron Road guide books, it is that you should not sit slavishly on the train, but that you should get off and explore the fascinating hinterland that the railway serves. We don't claim to be Egon Ronay, we are not the Scottish Mountaineering Club, we are not the local Chamber of Commerce, all the facilities and suggestions listed in this A-Z of the places served by the Far North and Kyle lines are simply ideas for you to develop. To the best of our knowledge the entries are accurate at the time of going to press, but we would urge you to use the telephone or the internet to check ahead for your own peace of mind. Make good use of the local Tourist Information Centres who are unfailingly enthusiastic and courteous models of patience and humour in the face of the most inane tourist enquiry.

## achanalt
*Map 18*

In addition to Captain Bertram Dickson, and the mausoleum of the Bignold family, the graveyard contains the remains of shepherds and postmasters.

## achnasheen
*Map 19*

Important road junction in the context of these wide open spaces

### accommodation
LEDGOWAN LODGE HOTEL - Tel: 01445 720252. Handsome former shooting box hotel 5 minutes walk from the station. Antlers over every door and an old-fashioned sense of courtesy and comfort. Hostel to rear for those on a budget. www.ledgownlodge.co.uk
CRAIG YOUTH HOSTEL - Tel: 01445 791284. Bunkhouse 2 miles east of station.

### eating & drinking
THE STUDIO - Tel: 01445 720227. Lively modern cafe adjunct to craft shop. Soups, salads and baked potatoes with an emphasis on organic ingredients.
*Non-residents also welcome at Ledgowan Lodge.*

### shopping
Post Office Stores - Tel: 01445 720241. Early closing Wednesdays and Saturdays. Closed Sundays.
THE STUDIO - see above. Jewellery workshop and gallery + crafts and gifts. www.studiojewellery.com

## achnashellach
*Map 19*

A back-packing launch pad for the Coulin Pass and Glen Torridon. Native pine woodland walks with the chance of seeing pine martens and golden eagles.

## alness
*Map 3*

Surprisingly busy little town, ranging along one main street. Road bridge by Thomas Telford and good walks along the banks of the River Averon. Annual Vintage & Classic Car Rally on the third Sunday in June.

### accommodation
COMMERCIAL HOTEL - High Street. Tel: 01349 882202. Small family run hotel with bar and lounge open to non-residents.

### eating & drinking
SPICE TANDOORI - High Street. Restaurant & takeaway. Tel: 01349 884400.
*Also Chinese and Balti takeaways and fish & chips.*

### shopping
Post office, supermarkets, banks with cash machines etc. Harry Gow bakery with cafe.

### things to do
HERITAGE CENTRE - High Street. Tel: 01349 883005. Enthusiastically developing conversion of former bakery to highlight local history and offer local information. Open daily ex Sundays. www.alness.com

### transport
TAXIS - Alness Hires. Tel: 01349 883700.
BUSES - Stagecoach services 25 & 25X shadow the railway between Inverness and Tain stopping at many villages which lost their railway stations circa 1960. Tel: 01463 239292.

## altnabreac
*Map 13*

As remote as they come, Altnabreac nevertheless boasts a primary school (though possibly no pupils!) and, about a mile east of the station, the exotic Lochdhu Lodge, a late Victorian pile whose zig-zag patterned rooftops and octagonal stairwell tower can be seen above the trees from the train. It dates from 1895 and has variously been a shooting lodge and an hotel. Good walks on well-made tracks to Forsinard and Scotscalder.

## ardgay
*Map 6*

Unremarkable railhead for Bonar Bridge.

### eating & drinking
THE LADY ROSS - all day cafe bar and restaurant, fish & chip takeaways. Tel: 01863 766315.

### shopping
Post Office (with cash machine) newsagents and general stores.

## attadale
*Map 21*

Slimline request stop south-east of Strathcarron set in a wonderful loch-side environment. Just get out and watch the tide ebb and flow and savour the smell of the gorse.

### things to do
ATTADALE GARDENS - Tel: 01520 722603. Waterfalls, rhododendron walks, kitchen garden and sunken garden, plus exotic species of plant on sale in nursery. www.attadale.com

## beauly
*Map 1*

First stop out from Inverness and tempting to go no further! Sweet little town centred on ruins of 13th century priory visited by Mary Queen of Scots. Impressive Boer War memorial in square.

### accommodation
LOVAT ARMS HOTEL - Tel: 01463 782313. Well-appointed, three star, family-run hotel with award-winning restaurant less than 5 minutes walk from station.
THE PRIORY HOTEL - The Square. Tel: 01463 782309. Comfortable three star hotel 6 minutes walk from station.

### eating & drinking
BEAULY COFFE SHOP - High Street. Tel: 01463 783379. Licenced restaurant for coffees, lunches and afternoon teas; open Mon-Sat.
*Plus Tandoori restaurant and Chinese takeaway and fish & chips. Also see hotels above for bar and restaurant meals and Made in Scotland below.*

### shopping
Post office, Alldays store, pharmacy. Baker, butcher, clothing, gifts and antiques shops.

### things to do
BEAULY FIRTH & GLENS TRUST - High Street. Tel: 01463 783444. Open daily. Excellent exhibitions and demonstrations relating to the locality. Gift shop with good choice of local literature.
MADE IN SCOTLAND - Station Road . Tel: 01463 782821. Retail outlet devoted to Scottish crafts and gifts. Gallery and restaurant. Open daily.

### transport
TAXIS - Beauly Taxis. Tel: 01463 782498.

## bonar bridge
*(Map 6)*

Its huge bow-string bridge seems too big for the village - it was built at a time when this was still the main road to the far north. Now Bonar is a quiet backwater, and because of the need to conserve salmon numbers, netting is no longer an enjoyable spectator sport.

### accommodation
BRIDGE HOTEL - Tel: 01863 766685. Homely 2 star hotel in village centre, 15 minutes walk from Ardgay station.
DUNROAMIN HOTEL - Tel: 01863 766236. Small hotel on the Lairg road. Bar and restaurant meals.

### eating & drinking
CALEDONIAN CURRY COMPANY - Tel: 01863 766025. Award-winning takeaways 10 minutes walk from Ardgay station. Kilt-lifting curries but also Scottish dishes such as venison in Black Isle beer. www.caledoniancurry.co.uk

# brora
Map 9

A *cause celebre* rocked Brora in 1910. In a plot of Dorothy Sayers like complexity, the owner of the Grand Hotel laid an elaborate trail of alibis - involving spurious train journeys and black of night bicycle rides - to deflect suspicion away from the fact that he had set the place on fire. Money, of course, lay at the route of this particular crime. The perpetrator was short of it, and needed the insurance. Finance still haunts Brora. In the words of June Tabor's song, 'all our trades have gone', but Brora stubbornly survives, a gutsy little town, with undoubtedly sharp elbows, but also a warm bosom well capable of cuddling holidaymakers and a fine centre for golfing and fishing. The beach is beautiful and you can expect to see seals, porpoises and otters in the rivermouth. Brora's history lists a bewildering roll-call of industries which have come and gone: coal mining, quarrying, salt-making, brick-making, engineering, herring fishing, woollen weaving, electricity generation. What a lively place it must have been. It even played its part in the Cold War by virtue of a MoD listening centre which operated until 1986. Yet all is not lost, for ice cream and whisky are still made in the town, and who could not live well on those alone?

## accommodation
ROYAL MARINE HOTEL - Golf Road. Tel: 01408 621252. Four star hotel originally built as a private home in 1913. Award-winning restaurant. 5 minutes walk from station. www.highlandescapehotels.com
THE LINKS HOTEL as above.
SUTHERLAND ARMS - Tel: 01408 621209. Modest, but comfortable, little hotel.

## eating & drinking
BRIDGE RESTAURANT - Tel: 01408 621327. Steaks, fish & chips, high teas and takeaways.
*Non-residents also welcome at the hotels above.*

## shopping
Post office, Co-op and Mace stores; pharmacy and newsagent. Bakery, butchers and Clydesdale Bank. Don't miss CAPALDI'S ice cream shop - Tel: 01408 621292.

## things to do
BRORA HERITAGE CENTRE - 8 minutes walk from station. Tel: 01408 622024. Open May - September. Friendly welcome and first rate displays of Brora's fascinating past.
CLYNELISH DISTILLERY - open April - October, Monday - Friday. Tel: 01408 623000. Just over a mile north-west of the station.

## transport
TAXIS - Wardle's. Tel: 01408 622222.
CAR HIRE - Russell's Garage, Gower Lane, 2 minutes walk from station. Tel: 01408 621356.

# culrain
Map 6

Montrose fought and lost a battle hereabouts in 1650, but the only violence you're likely to encounter now is that of back-packers trying to squeeze their gear on and off the train.

**Harbour view at Brora**

## accommodation
CARBISDALE CASTLE - Tel: 0871 330 8509. Grandiose mock castle dating from 1911, redefines the term Youth Hostel. Open March - October. 5 minutes walk from the station.

# dingwall
Map 2

Historic town where the real Macbeth - who wasn't half as bad as Shakespeare painted him - is reputed to have been born. A good base for those wishing to explore both the Far North and Kyle routes. Here and there some fine buildings, especially the ecclesiastical architecture, which gets off to a good start with the impressive Free Church outside the station, a pink sandstone structure in French Gothic style. Neil M. Gunn, the Scottish novelist, lived in the countryside above Dingwall for twelve years, writing many of his best known books here. A memorial in the hills to the north-west of the town commemorates this fact.

## accommodation
NATIONAL HOTEL - Tel: 01349 862166. Les Routiers recommended hotel within 2 minutes walk of the station.
TULLOCH CASTLE HOTEL - Tel: 01349 861325. 4 star country house hotel 2 miles north of station. www.tullochcastle.co.uk

## eating & drinking
THE STATION - Tel: 01349 865894. Cosy tearoom located in former ladies waiting room serving coffees, light lunches and teas, Monday - Saturday 10am-4pm. Also sells a good selection of books and crafts, including attractive prints and postcards of Dingwall station by local artist Janis Mennie. www.thestation.co.uk
THE MALLARD - Tel: 01349 866286. Modern diner/bar on down platform. All day menu.
DINGWALL TANDOORI - High Street. Tel: 01349 861917. Open daily for lunch and dinner.
*Also worth walking to the far end of High Street for RENATO'S Italian fish & chips and ice cream.*

## shopping
All facilities available within easy reach of the station. MERCAT BOOKS on Church Street is worth half an hour of any self-respecting bookworm's time - Tel: 01349 865593. Model railway fans will be attracted to the SPORTS & MODEL SHOP on High Street.

## things to do
DINGWALL MUSEUM - High Street. Tel: 01349 865366. Open Monday - Saturday, May to September. Local history nicely housed in the Old Toll Booth.
MCDONALD MONUMENT - 10 minutes walk from the station at the top of Green Hill, though first you must obtain the key from the council office on Burn Place, which will double the time. Well worth the effort, however, for the views from the top!

## walking
The excellent 'Mid-Ross Path Network' encourages walkers and cyclists to explore Dingwall's hinterland. Path 1 (3 miles) explores the Dingwall Canal and includes the Ferry Picnic Site which offers fine views over Cromarty Firth. Leaflets available locally.

## transport
TAXIS - C&E Taxis. Tel: 01349 862412.
BUSES - hourly Stagecoach links to/from Strathpeffer. Tel: 01463 239292.
CAR HIRE - Mackays, Tel: 01349 865366.

## dornoch
*(Map 9)*

Without a railway station since 1960, Dornoch is nevertheless worth inclusion in the gazetteer because it can be reached from Tain by bus, because it has a Blue Flag beach, and because it is simply very beautiful.

### accommodation
DORNOCH CASTLE - Tel: 01862 810216. Hugely comfortable and characterful hotel housed in 15th century Bishop's Palace. www.dornochcastlehotel.com
DORNOCH HOTEL - Tel: 01862 810351. Open March to November. Imposing hotel opened in 1904 by the Highland Railway. www.shearingsholidays.com
EAGLE HOTEL - Tel: 01862 810008. Small hotel with popular bar. www.eagledornoch.co.uk

### eating & drinking
THE COFFEE SHOP - Tel: 01862 810916. Lively modern internet cafe offering also Tourist Information and Bicycle Hire. www.jail-dornoch.com

### shopping
All facilities and not a supermarket in sight. Among many excellent outlets are: DORNOCH BOOKSHOP (Tel: 01862 810165) and the gifts, crafts, woollens, gallery shop JAIL - Tel: 01862 810555.

### things to do
HISTORYLINKS - Tel: 01862 811275. Open May to September, Monday to Saturday. If there's one thing the towns of the north-east Highlands do well it's interpreting their history, and this is one of the best at it. Special attention devoted to the Dornoch Light Railway. www.historylinks.org.uk

### transport
BUSES - Stagecoach service 25X runs hourly from Tain (Lamington Sq) Monday to Saturday. Tel: 01463 239292.

## duirinish
*Map 22*

Fifty-nine and three-quarter miles from Dingwall: lark-song, old surfacemen's cottages and a country mile to Duirinish itself, a gently sloping line of whitewashed crofts on either bank of a peaty burn.

## duncraig
*Map 21*

Tiny request stop tucked under a rocky (but bosky) headland on the lip of Plockton Bay. Well marked path along the water's edge to Plockton, or up through the woods past Duncraig Castle to CRAIG HIGHLAND FARM, a visitor centre for rare breeds where b&b is also available. Tel: 01599 544205.

## dunrobin castle
*Map 9*

Summer timetable only stop for the fabulous seat of the Sutherlands. In his day the 3rd Duke owned more land than anyone in Western Europe and was rich enough to indulge his passion for railways. The least you can do is repay his 'munificence and zeal' by de-training here and paying homage to this marvellous house, part Scotch castle, part French chateau, as Queen Victoria remarked. Other observers have noted the incongruity of its fairy tale appearance on the rim of the sea, but there's a lovely eccentricity about the castle which, in any case, pre-dates Barry's self-indulgence by five centuries. Oh yes, and the gardens are gorgeous too, and there are some fine walks to be had in the grounds ranging from quarter of an hour to two hours in duration. The castle is open to the public from April to October, generally from 10.30am Mon-Sat and noon on Sundays, last admissions being at 4pm early and late in the season and 5pm in high summer. Tel: 01408 633177. Museum, falcony, restaurant and gift shop.

## fearn
*Map 4*

Station for Hill of Fearn a mile to the east.

### accommodation
FEARN HOTEL - Tel: 01862 832234. Bar meals and B&B.

### shopping
General store and post office/butcher.

## forsinard
*Map 12*

Forsinard for Flow Country! Remote as it may be, this should almost be a compulsory stop on anyone's itinerary.

### accommodation
FORSINARD HOTEL - Tel: 01641 571221. Open March-January. Isolated yet comfortable hotel catering predominently for dry-fly fishermen and deer-stalkers, yet ideal for a quiet escape. Food for non-residents. www.theforsinard.co.uk

### things to do
RSPB FORSINARD - Tel: 01641 571225. Splendid nature reserve with small visitor centre housed in station building. CCTV links with hen-harriers nesting in season. Guided walks meet some of the trains - telephone to check - or self-guide yourself around the mile long Dubh Lochan Trail on which you'll encounter bog myrtle, sundew, sphagnum mosses, peat banks and the kind of birds which don't come to your bird-table back home.

## garve
*Map 17*

There is practically no reason for alighting at Garve: the shop has shut down and the hotel deals chiefly in coach parties!

## georgemas junction
*Map 14*

Isolated junction station whose former function is obsolete now that the train runs intact to both Thurso and Wick. It derived its name from a fair held hereabouts on St George's Day.

## golspie
*Map 9*

It may look glum on a dreich day when the 1st Duke has his head in the clouds, but Golspie repays perseverance, revealing itself an unprentious little seaside town where yours will often be the only footprints on the fine, sandy beach.

### accommodation
THE GOLF LINKS HOTEL - Tel: 01408 633408. Modest but comfortable 2 star hotel overlooking the sea near the station. www.golflinkshotel.co.uk
SUTHERLAND ARMS HOTEL - Tel: 01408 633234. 3 star hotel once compared by Telford to being the equal of anything in England. 15 minutes walk from the station.
BEN BHRAGGIE HOTEL - Tel: 01408 633242. Small hotel 12 minutes walk from station.

### eating & drinking
THE TRAWLER - Main Street. Tel: 01408 633869. Restaurant adjunct to fish & chip shop.
TWENTY TWENTY CAFE - Fountain Street. Tel: 01408 633022. Snacks and ice creams.
RAYMOND'S CHINESE TAKEAWAY - Main Street. Tel: 01408 633998.

### shopping
Co-op, post office, Bank of Scotland (with cash machine), gift shop, art gallery, fishmonger and pharmacy.

### things to do
ORCADIAN STONE COMPANY - Main Street. Tel: 01408 633483. Open Monday to Saturday, Easter to October. Fascinating exhibition of rocks, minerals and fossils. Gift shop.

### walking
Splendid centre for undemanding walks: the Ben Bhraggie Monument; Golspie Burn; Little Ferry.

### transport
TAXIS - Wardles. Tel: 01408 622222.

## helmsdale
*Map 10*

The harbour is heavenly, and as a base for exploring the seaboard, Strath Ullie and Glen Loth, Helmsdale could not be bettered. But there is scar tissue from the past still not fully healed, for the Helmsdale you see today is largely an early 19th century planned village, a consolation prize for crofters evicted during the clearances, who, it was hoped, would make a fresh start out of fishing. Certainly, the sea did provide a living, and at the height of the herring boom there were over two hundred boats using the harbour. Nowadays some eighteen families still earn their keep this way, concentrating on prawns and lobsters and seine netting haddock and cod with a small traditional fleet of vessels which provide attractive scenes in the harbour when landing their catches. The harbour walls, though, they'll tell you, are suffering from erosion, and major investment is required if they are not to crumble away. Up in the town itself, you'll see that the grid-pattern streets are named after the Sutherland's Staffordshire connections north to south, and their Scottish associations east to west. Look out for Thomas Telford's lovely river bridge of 1811, and the curious ice house nearby. More about Helmsdale can be discovered on its very good community website: www.helmsdale.org

### accommodation
BRIDGE HOTEL - Dunrobin Street. Tel: 01431 821100. Well-appointed hotel frequented by fishermen. Within easy reach of station. www.bridgehotel.net
YOUTH HOSTEL - Tel: 0871 330 8525. Inexpensive accommodation in former village hall. Open May to September.

Helmsdale -
La Mirage!

## eating & drinking

LA MIRAGE - Dunrobin Street. Tel: 01431 821615. Astonishment
is your first reaction to this uniquely and flamboyantly decorated
fish & chip restaurant - the creation of Barbara Cartland devotee,
Nancy Sinclair - followed by sheer enjoyment and an ardent wish
to return, just to check that you weren't dreaming!
BUNILLIDH RESTAURANT - Dunrobin Street. Tel: 01431 821457.
Specialises in locally caught seafood. B&B also available.
*Good bar and restaurant food also obtainable at the Bridge Hotel,
takeaways from both restaurants,and see Timespan below.*

## shopping

Post office, butcher, Spar, Mace & Cost-cutter stores. Bank of
Scotland with cash machine in Sutherland Street.

## things to do

STRATH ULLIE - Shore Street. Tel: 01431 821402. Crafts and local
information. Gold panning equipment for sale or hire.
TIMESPAN - Tel: 01431 821327. Open April to mid-October 9.30am-
5.00pm; from 2pm on Sundays. It would be difficult to overstate the
appeal of this splendid local heritage centre with its herb garden
and art gallery. A walk-through series of re-created rooms and
tableaux  illustrate Helmsdale's history in an imaginative way which
will please young and old alike. Really good gift shop and
cafe/restaurant too. Thoroughly recommended!
FISHING - the Bridge Hotel Tackle Shop will point you in the right
direction. Tel: 01431 821100.

## transport

TAXIS - MacLeod's, Tel: 01431 821234. Wardle's, Tel: 01431 821387.

## kildonan                                                    *Map 11*

Isolated request stop for gold panners!

## kinbrace                                                    *Map 11*

Request stop at the junction of the lonely road to Bettyhill.

## kyle of lochalsh                                            *Map 22*

The Skye Bridge opened in 1995, in the process robbing Kyle of
an important element of its romance. No longer - more's the pity
- are the sort of lads who are born to be king, carried across the
Kyle Akin strait by bonny boats resembling birds on the wing.
Though, if it's summer, and you're determined to reach Skye in the
traditional manner, you could hire a car and drive round to Glenelg,
where a ferry still operates across to Kylerhea.If the time at your
disposal, however, is curtailed by the railway timetable, then Kyle's
own attractions should be sufficient enough to sustain your interest.

## accommodation

LOCHALSH HOTEL - Tel: 01599 534202. Former railway hotel.
Past its heyday, perhaps, but comfortable enough, and well worth
patronising for the views from its rooms alone.
KYLE HOTEL - Tel: 01599 534204. Popular 3 star hotel in the
centre. www.kylehotel.co.uk
CUCHULAINN'S - Tel: 01599 534492. Backpacker's hostel on
Station Road.

## eating & drinking

THE SEAFOOD RESTAURANT -  Railway Station. Tel: 01599
534813. An atmospheric location and an imaginative menu make
this, arguably, the best venue for eating-out in Kyle. Open for
lunchtime baguettes, soups etc 10am-3pm; open for dinner from
6.30pm. www.the-seafood-restaurant.co.uk
THE WAVERLEY RESTAURANT - Main Street. Tel: 01599 534337.
Worth seeking out, an intimate little restaurant owned by a Dutch
lady.
JJ's - Tel: 01599 534248. Freshly cooked fish & chips.

## shopping

Banks, cash machines and a Co-op supermarket give Kyle a
deceptively metropolitan air. Good butchers and fishmongers. Gift
shops too, of course, and a selection of railway titles in the Pharmacy.

## things to do

TOURIST INFORMATION - Tel: 01599 534198/534390. (Seasonal)
KYLE STATION VISITOR CENTRE - Tel: 01599 534824. Museum,
gift shop, malt whisky centre and bike hire run by the Friends of
the Kyle Line. Open daily Mar-Nov, 11.15am-5.15pm.
SEAPROBE ATLANTIS - Ferry Pier. Tel: 0800 980 4846. Glass-
bottom boat trips to see shipwrecks, stunning scenery, otters, seals
and porpoises.

## transport

TAXIS - Kyle Taxi Company. Tel: 01599 534323.
CAR HIRE - as above.
BUSES -  service 55 operates on a half-hourly frequency daily
to/from Kyleakin on Skye with connections to/from Portree. No.60
runs hourly, Mon-Fri during the summer to the famous castle at
Eilean Donan. Tel: 01463 710555 or 0870 608 2 608.
THE SKYE FERRY (Glenelg-Kylerhea) - Tel: 01599 511302.
www.skyeferry.co.uk

## invergordon

Map 3

Its agreeably wide and spacious main street hints at a more significant past, but you sense that the heart has gone out of Invergordon.

### accommodation / eating & drinking

MARINE HOTEL -High Street. Tel: 01349 852419. Small hotel with lounge and public bars and a restaurant open to non-residents.

### shopping

Post office, Somerfield supermarket, banks, bakers etc.

### transport

TAXIS - Murrays. Tel: 01349 852555.

## inverness

Map 1

The Highland Capital seems positively metropolitan if you've just stepped off the train from the Far North. But as a point of departure for Wick, or Thurso, or Kyle the emphasis is reversed, and Inverness might well represent your last contact for some time with pavements and street lights and McDonalds.

### accommodation

ROYAL HIGHLAND HOTEL - adjacent railway station. Tel: 01463 231926. Imperious former railway hotel worth patronising for its plumbing alone. Just through the door, Robbie's convivial bar is ideal if you're waiting for the sleeper, whilst the restaurant with its Highland Railway coat of arms is satisfyingly austere. wwwroyalhighlandhotel.co.uk
GLEN MHOR HOTEL - Ness Bank. Tel: 01463 234308. 3 star hotel in fine location overlooking the river. Award-winning restaurant. www.glen-mhor.com
TRAVEL INN - Millburn Road. Lodge style accommodation which may appeal to railway enthusiasts owing to its location alongside Millburn Yard. Tel: 01463 712010. Adjoining restaurant housed in former distillery.
YOUTH HOSTEL - Victoria Drive. 7 minutes walk from the station off Millburn Road. Tel: 0871 330 8529. Considered one of the best in the UK, open all year round.

### eating & drinking

THE MUSTARD SEED - corner of Bank and Fraser streets. Tel: 01463 220220. Open 12-3pm and 6-10pm daily, this lively and modern riverside restaurant would not seem out of place in Edinburgh or Glasgow. Personable young staff serve memorable meals at surprisingly reasonable prices. www.themustardseedrestaurant.co.uk
QISMAT - Millburn Road. Tel: 01463 716020. Tandoori restaurant 2 minutes from station. www.quismat.co.uk
BLACKFRIARS - Academy Street. Tel: 01463 233881. CAMRA recommended pub usually featuring Black Isle Brewery ales. Home-cooked and inexpensive food plus live entertainment most evenings. www.blackfriars.50megs.com
LEAKEY'S - Church Street. Cafe serving soups and open sandwiches, cakes etc on inside balcony overlooking shelves and shelves of secondhand books. Tel: 01463 239947.

CLACHNAHARRY INN - Tel: 01463 239806. Convivial coaching inn overlooking the railway and the canal. About 20 minutes walk from the city centre but worth it. Open all day, families welcome, good bar meals and Scottish beers.

### shopping

The compact city centre means that everything's within 'rushing back for your train' distance of the station. High Street and Bridge Street are the main thoroughfares - the former being pedestrianised. Elsewhere, highlights include the VICTORIAN MARKET tucked away between the shop fronts on Academy Street, Union Street and Queensgate and readily visible from the Station Square. The market's uncanny railway-like architecture dates from 1891, the result of extensive rebuilding after a fire. Also on Union Street you might look out for THE GOURMET'S LAIR, a delicatessen offering some nice lines in local food and drink. Bookworms should make a bee line for LEAKEY'S on Church Street, reputedly Scotland's largest secondhand and antiquarian bookseller. The extended EASTGATE CENTRE is well located for the railway station, and there's a large branch of SAFEWAY nearby as well.

### things to do

TOURIST INFORMATION - Castle Wynd. Tel: 01463 234353.
MUSEUM & ART GALLERY - Castle Wynd. Tel: 01463 237114. www.invernessmuseum.com
MORAY FIRTH CRUISES - Shore Street. Tel: 01463 717900. April to September. Go and see the dolphins in the firth. Every hour and a half from 10.30am.
GUIDE FRIDAY - open top bus tours of Inverness, Culloden and Loch Ness. Regular departures from the railway station May to October - Tel: 01463 224000.

### transport

TAXIS - Central Highland Taxis. Tel: 01463 222222.
CAR HIRE - Thrifty Car Rental, Harbour Road, 7 minutes walk from the station but if you pre-book they'll meet you off the train, Tel: 01463 224466. Sharp's Reliable Wrecks, Tel: 01463 236684, office handily located on station concourse.
BUSES - Tel: 01463 239292. Bus station adjacent to railway station.
CYCLE HIRE - Highland Cycles, Telford Street. Tel: 01463 234789. Barneys, Castle Street - Tel: 01463 232249.

## invershin

Map 6

One half of that well-loved double-act 'Invershin & Culrain'. Splendid views across the Kyle of Sutherland to Carbisdale Castle. Access via footbridge to Forest Walks.

### accommodation

INVERSHIN HOUSE - Tel: 01549 421202. Accommodation and evening bar meals.

## lairg

'An ideal centre for those who wish to get about' in the words of the 1955 British Railways *Holiday Guide*. And though we like to think ourselves a tad too sophisticated merely to 'get about' now,

Lairg remains a 'frontier town', a cross-roads, strung-out, yet significant in the context of the wilder country on its doorstep, a post-bus inspired launch-pad for the far west.

### accommodation

THE NIP INN - Main Street, 20 minutes walk from station. Tel: 01549 402243. Small hotel with lounge bar and restaurant open to non-residents.

### eating & drinking

CROFTERS - Main Street. Homely licenced restaurant adjunct to caravan park. Tel: 01549 402447.

### shopping

Post office, Bank of Scotland with cash machine, Mace, Spar and pharmacy. Tweeds, gifts and religious books.

### things to do

FERRYCROFT - Tel: 01549 402160. Open April to October, admission free. Exhibitions and interpretations of natural and historical matters, archaeological trail and woodland walk, plus tourist information. 15 minutes walk from the station.
FALLS OF SHIN - Tel: 01549 402231. Spectacular salmon leap and visitor centre 3 miles south of station via pedestrian suspension bridge; 5 miles by road. Restaurant and Harrod's gift shop.

### transport

BUSES - Macleod's Coaches meet most trains and will ease your passage to the village centre. Tel: 01408 641354.
POSTBUS - connections to the far north and west: Durness, Lochinver, Altnaharra, Tongue etc. Tel: 08457 740740.
BICYCLE HIRE - Artfire pottery and coffee shop at Balloan (2 miles north-east of the railway station) offers cycle hire - Tel: 01549 402324.

## lochluichart

Map 18

Request stop for hydro-electric power enthusiasts.

## muir of ord

Map 2

Neat little sandstone village, formerly known as Tarradale before the coming of the railway, but frankly not of huge appeal to tourists.

### accommodation

ORD HOUSE HOTEL - Tel: 01463 870492. 2 star country house hotel. www.ord-house.com

### eating & drinking

AMRIG TANDOORI - Great North Road. Indian takeaway. Tel: 01463 871995.

### shopping

Banks with cash machines, Spar and butcher.

### things to do

GLEN ORD DISTILLERY - Tel: 01463 872004. Distillery tours Monday to Friday, also Saturdays from July to September. www.malts.com

### transport

TAXIS - MacGourlay's. Tel: 01463 870568.

## plockton
Map 21

An avuncular headland cushions Plockton from 'westlin winds' and the warm waters of the Gulf Stream bring a quasi-Mediterranean climate in their wake. *Bonhomie* thrives in the delightful setting, but Plockton's past is not so rosy, its origins belonging to the dark period of the clearances. Briefly it flourished as a centre for herring fishing, but was hit badly by the potato famine of 1846, not always solely an Irish tragedy. Crofting, however, survived, and indeed continues to, in a 21st century manner where there are often additional sources of income as well. Fishing (for prawns) and tourism complement such activities. The parish church of 1828 is the work of Thomas Telford.

### accommodation
THE PLOCKTON HOTEL - Tel: 01599 544274. Very comfortable family run hotel on the water's edge. 10 minutes walk downhill from station. www.plocktonhotel.co.uk
THE HAVEN HOTEL - Tel: 01599 544223. Very comfortable family run hotel not quite on the water's edge. 9 minutes walk downhill from the station. www.havenhotelplockton.co.uk
PLOCKTON INN - Tel: 01599 544222. Lively inn and seafood restaurant offering accommodation and traditional music evenings. www.plocktoninn.co.uk
PLOCKTON STATION BUNKHOUSE - Tel: 01599 544235. Highland Railway style signal box bunkhouse.

### eating & drinking
OFF THE RAILS - Tel: 01599 544423. Charming and sympathetic conversion of old station building into stylish 'all-day' cafe/restaurant. www.off-the-rails.co.uk

### shopping
PLOCKTON STORES & BUTTERY - Tel: 01599 544263. Post office and general store with cafe, internet access too. Also LOCH DUBH STORE which appeared in *Hamish Macbeth*.

### things to do
CALUM'S SEAL TRIPS - Tel: 01599 544306. Hugely enjoyable boat trips around the bay to see the seals (and maybe even an otter or two) every two hours from 10am-4pm throughout the season, but note that departure point alters with state of tide. Also special evening cruises.
BOAT HIRE - as above. Rowing boats and canoes.

### transport
TAXIS - Plockton Taxis, Tel: 01599 544389.
CYCLE HIRE - Tel: 01599 544255.

## rogart
Map 8

Visitors are apt to fall under Rogart's spell, and display a marked tendency to prolong their stay beyond the duration originally intended. There are no obvious visitor attractions, just a profound sense of peace and of responsibility unravelling.

### accommodation
SLEEPERZZZ - Tel: 01408 641343. Unusual, yet comfortable and enjoyable accommodation in railway carriages, a bus and a

**Sleeperzzz, Rogart**

showman's trailer. Discounts if you arrive by train. Guests have free use of bicycles. www.sleeperzzz.com

### eating & drinking
PITTENTRAIL INN - Tel: 01408 641353. Convivial Highland inn offering bar and restaurant meals.

### shopping
ROGART STORES - Tel: 01408 641200. Post office & Spar.

## scotscalder
Map 14

Not even a village to its name. Pleasant 3 mile walk westwards to see the standing stone on Ben Dorrery.

### accommodation
STATION - Tel: 0208 969 0882. Self-catering available in lovingly restored station building; each room decorated to a different period.

## stromeferry
Map 21

Once a vibrant point of embarkation for the ferry across Loch Carron, now bereft of almost any activity at all, and even the hotel has burnt down. Very sad ...

## strathcarron
Map 20

Railhead for Lochcarron on the opposite side of the water.

### accommodation / eating & drinking
STRATHCARRON HOTEL - Tel: 01520 722227. Comfortable and friendly lineside inn offering accommodation, food and some good Scottish beers. Open 11am-11pm daily and CAMRA recommended.

### shopping
Post Office Store (with tourist information and internet access) housed in former station building. Tel: 01520 722218.

### things to do
LOCHCARRON SMITHY HERITAGE CENTRE - Tel: 01520 722722. Open Monday to Saturday, April to October. 25 minutes walk from Strathcarron station. Blacksmith's forge, local history and pottery. www.balnacra.com/smithy.htm

### transport
CAR, BIKE, BOAT HIRE - Ross Rentals, Tel: 01520 722205.

## strathpeffer
(Map 17)

Not presently on the rail network, but may one day rise phoenix-like from the ballast of its branchline's disused trackbed. An elegant spa town, worth considering as a base if you're not totally reliant on the trains.

### accommodation
BEN WYVIS HOTEL - Tel: 01997 421323. 2 star hotel. www.british-trust-hotels.com
HIGHLAND HOTEL - Tel: 01997 421457. 3 star hotel. www.shearingsholidays.com

### things to do
HIGHLAND MUSEUM OF CHILDHOOD - Tel: 01977 421031. Open April to October. Coffee shop. Fascinating museum housed in former railway station. www.hmoc.freeserve.co.uk

## tain

*Map 5*

Tain was a place of pilgrimage in the Middle Ages, on account of it being the birthplace circa 1000 of St Duthac. King James IV was a regular visitor, hence King's Causeway remains the name of the road from the south. Robert the Bruce sent his family here in 1306 to keep them safe from the English, but they were betrayed. In 1650 Montrose spent the night here on his way to Edinburgh to be executed. Such startling historical occurrences seem at odds with soporific Tain now, for it has mellowed into a quiet resort on Dornoch Firth, small town Scotland personified.

### accommodation

MANSFIELD HOUSE HOTEL - Tel: 01862 892052. Imposing Victorian hotel in own grounds about 10 minutes walk from the station. www.mansfieldhouse.eu.com
MORANGIE HOUSE HOTEL - Tel: 01862 892281. Comfortable 3 star hotel on northern outskirts of town, 10 minutes walk from the station.

### eating & drinking

BRAMBLES - King Street. Tel: 01862 892929. Coffee shop and crafts.
KANISHA - St Duthas Street. Tel: 01862 893003. Indian restaurant and takeaway.
CAFE VOLANTE - Tel: 01862 892101. Fish & chips and ice cream, a typical Scots cafe.

### shopping

Four banks (3 with cash machines), two pharmacies, two bakeries, one butcher and one bookshop. Several craft shops, a convenience store and a Co-op supermarket on the northern outskirts. BROWN'S GALLERY features contemporary Scottish art - Tel: 01862 893884.

### things to do

TAIN THROUGH TIME - Tel: 01862 894089. Open Monday to Saturday, April to October. Really interesting audio-enhanced tour of Tain's rich history.
GLENMORANGIE DISTILLERY - Tel: 01862 892477. Open Monday to Friday all year round, Saturdays and Sundays in June to August. Delve into the traditions of the 'Sixteen Men of Tain'. www.glenmorangie.com

### transport

BUSES - Stagecoach service 25X provides useful hourly, Mon-Sat link with Dornoch. Tel: 01463 239292.

## thurso

*Map 15*

Not only *is* Thurso the northernmost town in the UK, it *feels* like it. Not in a derogatory sense, but in as much as you feel like you are about to fall off the edge of things, as if, in the old cartographic convention, there will be serpents in the waves beyond Thurso's broad and inviting beach. Essentially there are two Thursos: the old medieval hotchpotch of streets near the harbour-mouth; and the newer, grid-pattern part of town leading down from the station which dates from the end of the 18th century. This latter was the brain-child of Sir John Sinclair (1754-1835) known in his day as 'the most indefatigable man in Britain'. His statue adorns the square

of the same name. The older part of town is characterised by a dysfunctional pattern of streets, and sudden encounters with enigmatic buildings such as the old kippering-house in Shore Street and a circular towered house dated 1686. But sooner or later you reach The Esplanade, built in 1882, and here the urge will come over you to rip off your socks and shoes and run out across the sands to the sea. Do not even attempt to resist it!

### accommodation

THE STATION HOTEL - Tel: 01847 892003. Small 3 star hotel with self-catering annex. Harry Lauder stayed here in 1906. 2 minutes walk from the station. www.stationthurso.co.uk
PENTLAND HOTEL - Tel: 01847 893202. Princes Street. Small 3 star hotel 5 minutes walk from the station.
ROYAL HOTEL - Tel: 01847 893191. Traill Street. Thurso's largest hotel, 3 star rating. 5 minutes walk from station. www.british-trust-hotels.com
SANDRA'S HOSTEL - Tel: 01847 894575. Backpacker's hostel within easy reach of station. Bikes for hire. www.sandras-backpackers.ukf.net

### eating & drinking

LE BISTRO - Tel: 01847 893737. Traill Street. Atmospheric restaurant, not open Sundays and Mondays.
CHARLIE CHAN - Tel: 01847 890888. Chinese restaurant and takeaway on Sinclair Street.

### shopping

All services. Safeway and Co-op supermarkets. Model railway enthusiasts might like to have a peep in DURRAN'S on Sir John's Square, its crafts and gifts will keep the ladies happy while you choose a congratulatory souvenir, from their good stocks of the latest Bachmann and Hornby models, to mark your rail ride to the north.

### things to do

TOURIST INFORMATION - Tel: 01847 892371. Riverside - open throughout the season.

### transport

TAXIS - Thurso Taxis, Tel: 01847 893031. Meiklejohn Taxis, Tel: 01847 892827.
BUSES - Tel: 01847 893123. Services from the railway station to/from Scrabster for the Orkney Ferry. Also services to/from John O'Groats and other local destinations.
BICYCLE HIRE - Tel: 01847 894575.
FERRIES - Northlink services from Scrabster to Stromness on Orkney (crossing time 1 hour 30 minutes) Tel: 01865 851144.

## wick

*Map 16*

Murdoch Paterson's 1877 Bridge of Wick takes you from the station, over the Wick River, past the Town Hall and into the centre of town, an auspicious introduction to an architecturally and atmospherically fascinating, if now devitalised, town which can trace its origins back to Viking times. High Street leads to the Market Place, where the crow-stepped, Edwardian Post Office has suffered the indignity of becoming a pub. Thence you should proceed to the harbour, a complex of quays and piers disappointingly lacking in vessels

when one considers that in its 19th century heyday close on a thousand fishing boats would jostle for berthing space. At the beginning of the 19th century Thomas Telford was called in by the British Fisheries Society to develop the harbour and he created Pulteney Town along the south shore of the river, named after Sir William Pulteney. In its heyday the harbour here was lined with herring yards and cooperages. Archive photographs, of which Wick Heritage Centre has a huge collection, depict astonishing scenes of industry almost unimaginable today.

### accommodation

MACKAY'S HOTEL - Tel: 01955 602323. Union Street, 2 minutes walk from station. Comfortable, wedge-shaped, 3 star hotel. www.mackayshotel.co.uk
NORSEMAN HOTEL - Tel: 01955 603344. 2 star hotel near the town centre, 5 minutes walk from the station. www.british-trust-hotels.com

### eating & drinking

BORD DE L'EAU - Tel: 01955 604400. Market Street. French restaurant: full meals, light snacks, coffees, baguettes etc. Closed Mondays.

### shopping

All services. Safeway supermarket. SIMPSON'S holds a good stock of Scottish literature in the Market Place - Tel: 01955 603304.

### things to do

TOURIST INFORMATION - Tel: 01955 602956. Whitechapel Road.
WICK HERITAGE CENTRE - Tel: 01955 605393. Bank Row. Unsung, yet hugely enjoyable museum of local history. Brilliant photographic collection. Open Easter to October, Monday to Satruday, 10am-3.45pm.
PULTENEY DISTILLERY - Tel: 01955 602371. Tours by arrangement of the home of Old Pulteney. www. oldpulteney.com
CAITHNESS GLASS - Tel: 01955 602286. Open Monday to Saturday all year round, Sundays Easter to December. Glassmaking visitor centre, shop and restaurant.

### transport

TAXIS - Jimmy's Taxis, Tel: 01955 602727. Johnnie's Taxis, Tel: 01955 605041. Peter's Taxis, Tel: 01955 604850.
BUSES - regular services down the Caithness coast to Lybster and Dunbeath, and up to John O' Groats. Tel: 01847 893123.

# information

*Karen Tanguy*

## using this guide

Twenty-two, north facing, one inch to one mile maps portray the route of the Far North (1-16) and Kyle of Lochalsh (17-22) routes. Each map is accompanied by a running commentary on matters historical, topographical and related to railway operation. Emphasis is given to the northward or westward journey respectively, but the details are equally relevant for travel in the opposite direction. Towards the rear of the guide a gazetteer gives details of all the stations on the route. This gazetteer gives a brief summary of each place together with itemised information on places to eat and find accommodation, shopping facilities, visitor centres, things to do and useful contacts such as bus links, taxi services and tourist information centres. Where accuracy is essential to the planning of an itinerary you are urged to make contact by telephone to ensure you have up to the minute details.

## scheduled services

Day to day services on the Far North and Kyle of Lochalsh routes are operated by ScotRail. There are three services each way on weekdays between Inverness and Wick, with a fourth that carries early-morning commuters from Tain to Inverness; also three each way between Inverness and Kyle of Lochalsh with a fourth on that route in July and August. On Sundays one train each way covers both routes throughout the year with a second in July, August and September. The average journey time between Inverness and Thurso is three and a half hours (Wick four hours), between Inverness and Kyle of Lochalsh two and a half hours. Services are currently provided by comfortable 158 diesel units which provide standard class, non-smoking facilities. Catering trolley services are available on the majority of services.

## charter trains

One or two companies run charter trains and excursions over the Far North and Kyle of Lochalsh lines from time to time.
SRPS Railtours - Tel: 01698 263814 www.srps.org.uk
The Royal Scotsman - Tel: 0131 555 1344 www.royalscotsman.com
Travelsphere - Tel: 01858 410818 www.travelsphere.co.uk
Grampian Railtours - Tel: 01358 789513
Highland Railway Heritage - Tel: 01397 722295

## tickets and travelpasses

There are ScotRail booking offices at Inverness, Dingwall, Thurso, Wick and Kyle of Lochalsh. A range of tickets is available from these offices and from the guards on board the trains. For an idea of fares (including current offers, Travelpasses etc) telephone **National Rail Enquiries on 08457 484950** or visit ScotRail's website at www.scotrail.co.uk
Tickets in advance are also obtainable from **ScotRail Telesales & Bookings. Tel: 08457 550033.**

## bicycles

Bicycles are conveyed free of charge on ScotRail service trains. The diesel units which provide the timetabled services over the Far North and Kyle of Lochalsh lines can convey just two bicycles per two car unit. Reservations are therefore *compulsory* and should be made at principal staffed stations or ScotRail Telesales on 08457 550033 up to eight weeks in advance but no later than two hours before the train *commences* its journey.

## further reading

The Highland Railway by H.A.Vallance ISBN 1 899863 07 9
The Skye Railway by John Thomas ISBN 0 946537 62 3
Rails to Kyle of Lochalsh by David McConnell ISBN 0 85361 513 6
Railway Holiday in Scotland by Michael Pearson ISBN 0 907864 90 2

## useful contacts

HIGHLAND RAIL PARTNERSHIP - Lairg Station, Sutherland IV27 4EX Tel: 01549 402896. Email railzzz@btinternet.com
BRITRAIL - rail travel in Britain exclusively for overseas visitors. Very affordable and flexible rail travel options such as the **BritRail** and **Freedom of Scotland** Travel Passes. Visit: www.BritRail.net or call toll-free 1-877-677-1066 in USA and Canada.
HIGHLANDS OF SCOTLAND TOURIST BOARD, Strathpeffer, Ross-shire IV14 9HA. Tel: 01997 421160. Website: www.highlandfreedom.com
FRIENDS OF THE FAR NORTH LINE - www.fofnl.org.uk
FRIENDS OF THE KYLE LINE - Tel: 01599 534824.
HIGHLAND RAILWAY SOCIETY - www.hrsoc.org.uk
SMALL STATIONS SOCIETY - Tel: 0208 969 0882.
NATIONAL RAIL ENQUIRIES - Tel: 08457 484950.

## acknowledgements

Wayzgoose extend grateful appreciation to the following individuals and bodies who have helped so much with the production of this guide: Frank Roach and Chris Kendall of the Highland Rail Partnership; John Yellowlees, Alan Dougall, Bruce Penman, Donald McKenzie and Philip Macrae of ScotRail; John Macfarlane, former Kyle line observation car commentator; David Voisey and Mrs Katherine Grant of Kyle; John Allison of the Highland Council; Geoffrey Evison of Berwick; the Small Stations Society; the Friends of the Far North Line and the Friends of the Kyle Line. Special thanks to Jackie Pearson, Karen Tanguy, Giampiero Lo Giudice and all at STIGE!

## uncaptioned photographs

Front cover: The Shin or Oykel Viaduct.
Back cover: Kyle of Lochalsh. This page: Barrow-boy, Rogart.